ASPERGER'S
TEENS

Understanding
High School for
Students on the
Autism Spectrum

by
BLYTHE GROSSBERG, PsyD

Magination Press • Washington, DC
American Psychological Association

to John and Teddy—*BG*

Published by
MAGINATION PRESS®
An Educational Publishing Foundation Book
American Psychological Association
750 First Street, NE
Washington, DC 20002

Magination Press is a registered trademark of the American Psychological Association.

For more information about our books, including a complete catalog, please write to us, call 1-800-374-2721, or visit our website at www.apa.org/pubs/magination.

Printed by Lake Book Manufacturing, Inc., Melrose Park, IL

Cover design and illustrations by Naylor Design, Inc., Washington, DC

Library of Congress Cataloging-in-Publication Data
Grossberg, Blythe N.
  Asperger's teens : understanding high school for students on the autism spectrum/by Blythe Grossberg, PsyD Ma.
    pages cm
  Includes bibliographical references and index.
  ISBN 978-1-4338-1919-3 — ISBN 1-4338-1919-8 1. Youth with autism spectrum disorders—Education (Secondary) 2. Autism in adolescence.
3. Asperger's syndrome in adolescence. I. Title.
  LC4717.5.G76 2016
  371.9—dc23
                            2014031643

CONTENTS

INTRODUCTION

If you have Asperger's, also sometimes referred to as Asperger's Syndrome or high-functioning autism and officially known as autism spectrum disorder (ASD) in the medical world, you may find that high school is a time of great promise and opportunity for you. You will have the chance to study topics that you are really excited about and learn more about academic subjects you are interested in. Students in high school are generally more tolerant towards other kids and more accepting of different types of styles and personalities than kids in middle school are.

On the other hand, you may also find that you can't always feel comfortable in high school. While you may be interested in learning and making friends, you may find that there are distractions and obstacles that get in your way. Some of these distractions may be external, such as too much noise in the lunchroom or hallways or confusing discussions in class. Some may be internal, such as feeling uninterested in what's going on in class or feeling more drawn to video games and the virtual world or to other hobbies such as reading or music than to what's going on around you. This book can help you use your strengths and unique personal style to feel more comfortable in high school.

HOW TO USE THIS BOOK

The goal of this book is to help you find your **comfort zone**—a comfortable place that is both physical and emotional in nature. That is, this book will help you find ways to feel comfortable in your classrooms and with friends as well as ways to make your body feel comfortable and safe. You will also think about how to feel more comfortable and relaxed in your mind.

This book is filled with strategies, or methods, to help you find that comfort zone. Some strategies involve changing your environment, while others involve changing the way you think. In this book, you will read about ways to help yourself act differently and think differently in school, all with the goal of making yourself feel more comfortable, more relaxed, and better able to make friends, understand teachers, and get the grades you are capable of. However, you may also decide that you don't have to think or act differently in certain situations—there are many things that you are comfortable with already and you have lots of strengths. This book will help to determine when to stick to what you know and what you are already good at doing.

Feel free to choose the strategies that you think will work best for you. At the end of each chapter, you will decide which goals you would like to set. In a way, setting goals is like playing video games—when you go on a quest in a role-playing game, for example, you can decide how to reach your ultimate destination or where you want to go—and you can choose how to use the skills or tools you possess to get to your destination. You also set goals when you decide to learn more about a subject that interests you, whether it is astronomy, music, or manga. Before we start on the quest of finding a comfortable place in high school, we are going to look at what Asperger's is and examine whether or not you feel comfortable revealing that you have Asperger's to other people. The answer to this question is entirely up to you.

UNDERSTANDING ASPERGER'S

Asperger's is something you are born with, and while each person with Asperger's is different, many people with Asperger's have the following similarities. Do any of these statements apply to you?

- Interest in words and a large vocabulary
- An interest in one subject or a few subjects that tends to be very strong
- Difficulty becoming interested in subjects that aren't your passion
- Sometimes, difficulty understanding how other people feel
- Sometimes, difficulty following conversations, particularly group conversations
- Sometimes, difficulty understanding people's facial expressions or **body language**, meaning how they communicate using their body
- Sometimes, feeling overwhelmed or anxious, particularly if there are a lot of people or a lot of noise
- Sometimes, difficulty asking for help from teachers and other adults
- An interest in connecting to other people but sometimes a feeling of confusion about how to do so

- Sometimes, difficulty making transitions from one activity to the next
- Sometimes, difficulty relaxing, eating a full and balanced diet, and getting enough sleep

While people with Asperger's may not follow this profile, many of them share some or all of these strengths and traits. This means that they have real strengths in areas of their interest. They may need help connecting to others but can do so with some strategies, or help. This book will provide you with some ideas about how you can use your strengths to your advantage and how you can use your strengths to help you in other areas.

Many people with Asperger's have incredible strengths.

Many people with Asperger's have incredible strengths. For example, they can often imagine worlds, artworks, scientific theories, and works of literature that no one else can. Experts believe that Asperger's can create a sense of being a visionary, meaning that you can create something entirely new—whether an actual work such as art or literature, or an idea such as a theory. For example, recent research from the Harvard Business School suggests that people with Asperger's have the necessary concentration, intelligence, and precision to make great software testers.[1]

---

[1]Lagace, M. (2008, April 14). The surprising right fit for software testing. *HBS Working Knowledge*. Retrieved from http://hbswk.hbs.edu/item/5869.html

People with Asperger's often have the ability to catch software bugs or problems that other people in the technology field do not detect. This is only one area in which people with Asperger's can excel. There are many fields in which people with Asperger's can be successful.

It's up to you to decide how to define yourself—both to yourself and the outside world.

You may not want to classify yourself as someone with Asperger's, and that is fine. It's up to you to decide how to define yourself—both to yourself and the outside world. However, it may be helpful for you to understand a bit more about Asperger's as you get older because this understanding may help you better comprehend yourself and the way your mind works, and it may help you explain yourself to others. You may want to consult the books and websites in the "Resources" section at the end of the book to learn more about Asperger's and read books by people who have written

Consult the books and websites in the "Resources" section at the end of the book to learn more about Asperger's.

about their experiences growing up and entering the work world while having Asperger's. Many famous and successful people have Asperger's, and reading their stories may provide you with inspiration and ideas about your life and future.

SHOULD YOU REVEAL THAT YOU HAVE ASPERGER'S?

The question about whether or not to tell your friends, classmates, and teachers that you have Asperger's is a difficult one, and each person has to make up his or her mind about whether to do so. You can also decide to tell a select group of friends and teachers, not all of them.

Here are some of the pros, or advantages, of revealing that you have Asperger's to your friends and teachers:

- They will understand why you struggle in certain areas, such as understanding classroom discussions, so they won't think you are trying to be deliberately rude or that you are trying to get the conversation off track.
- Teachers may be better able to understand how to help you if you describe what gets in your way and how some of these obstacles come from having Asperger's.
- Your school may be able to grant you certain **accommodations,** or changes in the school day, such as sitting in the front row so you can better pay attention to the teacher, taking tests with additional time to allow you to express your thoughts fully, using a computer for essay tests if you have illegible handwriting, permission to sit in a quiet place or take a break during the day if you are feeling overwhelmed, or other help—if you explain that you have Asperger's. You will need

a doctor, psychologist, or other professional to document that you have Asperger's to ask for this type of help, so be sure to work with your guidance counselor and parent if you want to request accommodations at school.

• Some of your friends and teachers will appreciate your honesty, and telling them about yourself may help you feel more comfortable with yourself. Start by telling one or two trusted friends and a teacher who you think are understanding before telling all of your friends and teachers. You may decide to tell only a select group of people about your Asperger's—you don't have to tell everyone.

Here are some of the cons, or negatives, about revealing that you have Asperger's to your friends and teachers:

• They may think you are like stereotypes, or general ideas they have about people with Asperger's—for example, being a computer wizard—even if you are not like that, and they may not understand or appreciate all the aspects of your personality.
• They may tend to think that you are not capable of doing certain things, though you are.
• You may prefer to be private about yourself, which is your right.

Now, take a few minutes to think about the pros and cons of revealing that you have Asperger's to your friends and teachers. You may want to write them down in two columns on a separate sheet of paper. Reviewing the list of pros and cons can help you decide whether to reveal you have Asperger's, and to whom.

If you are struggling with how to present yourself to your teachers and how to explain how Asperger's affects you, an organization called OASIS (on the web at http://www.aspergersyn drome.org) provides a teacher's guide that you can hand to your teachers and coaches to help them understand what Asperger's is and how they can help you. Feel free to use the OASIS handout as a guide that you can change or customize so that it best describes you and your needs. You can also present this guide to your guidance counselor and discuss with that person how to approach your teachers to let them know more about Asperger's. Your guidance counselor or another trusted adult can help you figure out the words to use when talking about Asperger's with your teachers and can help you figure out how and when to approach your teachers.

You may also be able to let your friends, classmates, and teachers know about you without *revealing that you have Asperger's.*

You may also be able to let your friends, classmates, and teachers know about you *without* revealing that you have Asperger's. Again, you may want to consult with your guidance counselor before approaching your teachers. For example, you can say something to a teacher similar to the following:

"I wanted to speak to you a little bit about how I can work best in your classroom. I am really interested in your subject, and I like to talk about things. However, I may sometimes get off track, so please let me know by touching me on the shoulder if I get really off track."

Having some traits that are related to Asperger's is only one part of your personality. Read on to discover more about how to understand the different parts of yourself and how to present these dimensions of yourself to others.

1

WHO ARE YOU? CREATING A PERSONAL PROFILE

Strengths are like tools you can bring out of a tool box to use to help yourself in everyday life. Each person has different strengths. For example, some kids are talented musicians, while others love doing math problems. In this chapter, you will think about what your strengths are and how well you recognize them and can use them. In the process, you will create a personal profile, or a list of your strengths and what you need to work on. The process of creating this profile will help you understand yourself better and enable you to take the next steps towards achieving your goals.

QUIZ YOURSELF!
HOW WELL DO YOU UNDERSTAND AND EXPLAIN YOURSELF?

Answer the following questions (don't worry—this is a fun quiz all about you) and then read on to figure out how well you understand what you can offer and how well you explain yourself to other people. For each question, choose the answer choice that best describes you:

1. When people ask me what my strengths are, I:
   a. Don't understand what they are talking about.
   b. Basically know what I am *not* good at, but don't know what I'm good at.
   c. I can explain what I'm good at and what I need to work on.
2. When my parents tell me that I need to work on developing my academic and social goals, I:
   a. Don't really understand what that means.
   b. Understand that when I was smaller, I had to work on social skills, but now that I'm older and in high school, I'm not really sure which goals I should have.
   c. Understand that I have certain strengths that I can use in school and elsewhere and that I can ask for help in areas that I'm not as strong in.
3. Each year in school, I:
   a. Don't think too much about what I'm achieving.
   b. Face the same obstacles again and again, though I am thinking about how to get help.
   c. Decide to set a goal about what I want to accomplish and work with my teachers to achieve it.
4. When I am struggling in an activity, I:
   a. Decide to stop doing it.
   b. Think about asking for help, though I don't always know where to turn to get help.
   c. Ask a teacher, parent, or friend for help or another way to approach the problem.

5. When I am asked to describe my interests, or what I like to do, I:
   a. Really don't know how to answer.
   b. Answer the same way each time, even though I'm not sure I'm describing myself fully.
   c. Am able to describe some of my real interests and explain why I'm interested in them.

How to score yourself:

If you answered mostly "a": You have real strengths, but you may not always understand what they are. In addition, you may at times need to learn how to explain how your mind works to teachers, parents, and friends and learn how to ask for help in areas in which you are not as strong. Understanding yourself will help you navigate the world of high school while feeling more comfortable and secure.

If you answered mostly "b": You understand some of your strengths and are starting to think about asking for some help from parents, teachers, and friends. You may not realize that people around you can provide more extensive or complete help than you are now getting, such as helping you think about different ways to approach a situation or problem. Learning how to ask for this type of help will help you feel more comfortable learning and making friends in high school.

If you answered mostly "c": You are doing a good job understanding what you do well and how to ask for help. Read on to find other ways to build on your strengths and learn how to do better with the help of others around you.

UNDERSTANDING YOUR STRENGTHS AND OBSTACLES

Before we think about how you can make yourself feel more comfortable in school, take an inventory of what you do well—and what you need to improve. Taking an inventory is similar to assessing which strengths or skills your character possesses in a role-playing video game, or determining the unique personality, behavior, or characteristics of a protagonist in a book. Each character is unique and has some strengths and lacks others; similarly, you have some unique strengths and some strengths you may need to acquire or develop.

Take an inventory of what you do well—and what you need to improve.

Another useful way to think about taking an inventory is to pretend you are packing for a trip to the beach. Before you leave for your trip, you must think about what you need to bring on your journey. Do you have a bathing suit? Do your flip-flops still fit? What about sunscreen or sunglasses? While packing, you take stock (or an inventory) of what you already have and think about what you still need to acquire.

Now is the time to think about your strengths. What skills or talents do you have that you consider to be strengths? What things can you do well? What are other skills that you would like to have?

Your Strengths

Think about your top three strengths. Jot them down on a separate sheet of paper to help you remember them. These can be related to school, such as "I'm good at understanding how to do research on the web," or they can be other qualities such as "I'm good at working with small children." Whatever you choose is up to you; if you are stuck, ask a trusted friend or a parent or teacher to help you.

WHAT DO I DO IF ...

Question: I really don't know what my strengths are. What do I do?
Answer: Try thinking about what other people, such as your teachers or other kids, say you do well. You can also think about your interests because areas of interest can often represent strengths. For example, if you are interested in astronomy, you may be motivated to learn more about it and may know a lot about this subject. If you are really stuck and can't come up with any strengths, ask a friend or adult you trust what he or she thinks your main strengths are.

Strengths You Need

Spend some time thinking of strengths you would like to have for school and for your social life that you don't yet have. The strengths you need are similar to skills you would like to acquire in a role-playing video games or items that you need to get to prepare for taking a trip. You can think of things like, "I would like to learn how to be better organized," or "I would like to find ways to make more friends in school." If you are stuck and can't think of anything, work with a trusted friend, parent, or teacher to come up with an answer that sounds right to you. You could add these strengths you need to your written list, too.

Your Obstacles

Now, think about what is getting in the way of your developing the strengths you would like to have but don't yet possess. These are obstacles that are similar to what you might find in a video game—things that prevent your character from advancing to the next level. Your obstacles can be internal barriers, meaning that they come from within yourself, such as, "I get frustrated when I try to work on something very hard," or they can be external factors such as, "I want to finish my homework, but I just don't have a quiet place to study." You will refer to these obstacles later, at the end of the chapter, in order to develop goals or what you want to achieve. Don't worry if you aren't quite sure yet about how to work around these obstacles. This book will give you some more information and strategies to help you start thinking about how to work on your obstacles. Now, note three obstacles on a separate sheet of paper.

CREATING YOUR PERSONAL PROFILE

Look at the list of strengths you already have, the list of strengths you need, and the list of your obstacles. Can you use these three lists to develop a few sentences about yourself? One easy way to do this is to take the strengths you have and the strengths you need and turn them into full sentences.

You can use the following as a guide, though you don't need to stick to it:

I am a person who likes _____ (fill in the strengths that you wrote down earlier here). My other talents are_____ (fill in other strengths). While I have a lot of strengths, I would like to develop certain areas, including _____(fill in two or three strengths you want to develop here from the list you created). What often gets in my way is _____ (fill in your obstacles from your earlier list here).

For example, if the strengths you have were "working well with children," "cooking," and "drawing anime characters," and the strengths you need were "becoming more organized," "learning to ask for help," and "learning to handle frustration," you can write something like the following:

"I am a person who enjoys babysitting and works well with children. My other talents are cooking and drawing, particularly anime characters. While I have a lot of talents, I would like to develop certain areas. I need to work on becoming more organized, learning to ask for help, and learning to handle frustration. What often gets in my way is that I think I should be perfect at all times."

Everyone has both strengths and weaknesses, though different ones, in their profiles.

While it may seem redundant to turn your lists of strengths you have and those you need into full sentences, this personal statement will help you present yourself to teachers, and it will help you formulate goals. It is helpful to know how to describe your **profile**, meaning your list of skills, strengths, and weaknesses, and it may help you to know that everyone has both strengths and weaknesses, though different ones, in their profiles. In other words, everyone has some strengths that they carry with them and that can help them get through parts of high school life that are more difficult for them.

BUILDING ON YOUR STRENGTHS

One of the reasons that it's important to understand the strengths you already have is that you can apply these strengths to the strategies in this book. This will help you find a comfortable place in high school and connect with friends and teachers. Here are some ways you may be able to apply your strengths:

You can apply your strengths to the strategies in this book.

- If you are an avid reader, you can read more about Asperger's and how people with Asperger's have used their strengths to their advantage. To find books, refer to the "Resources" section at the end of this book.
- If you are good with computer games, you can understand the idea of having strengths because it is similar to the tools or skills that your character carries with him or her in a quest. You, like characters in role-playing games, carry certain skills that will help you on your quest to feel more comfortable and connect with friends and teachers in high school.
- If you are comfortable speaking to adults, you will find it easier to approach your teachers for help. But, if you aren't comfortable, don't worry—this book will help you think about some ways to approach your teachers in a way that's comfortable for you.

Now, take a minute to look at your strengths, and try to think about how they might help you find a more comfortable place for yourself in high school and connect with friends and teachers. For example, if you are a musician, you can connect with people through orchestra or band, or if you are an artist, you can draw pictures for your teachers or other students. If you are stuck, speak with a trusted friend, parent, or teacher.

SETTING GOALS

Now, it's time to set some personal goals, as you might when starting a video game. Setting goals allows you to take small, manageable steps to reach where you want to go. While you may not be able to reach your final goal right away, by setting realistic steps, you can start the process of moving in the direction you want. To help you reach your goals, make them SMART in nature; that is:

Specific,
Measurable,
Attainable,
Realistic, and
Timely.

Let's look at each component of attainable goals. First, a goal must be specific. So, a goal that sets a certain target, such as, "I will find one extra-curricular activity this semester" is more specific than "I will find something to do after school."

A goal must be measurable, as is the goal above to "find one extra-curricular activity this semester." A goal such as "I will just be better at activities" isn't really as measurable because it's hard to know if you've achieved it.

The best kinds of goals are attainable. For example, you may want to become president of your school class, but that goal may or may not be attainable. While it's not a good idea to be defeatist, you may want to set a goal such as "I will run for student council," which you know you can achieve, as the results of the election are in part out of your control.

Similarly, the best goals are realistic—that is, you can reach them with a reasonable amount of effort in a relatively short period of time. For example, writing a best-selling book may not be doable in the short term, but you may be able to set a realistic goal such as "submitting an article to the school newspaper or literary magazine this semester."

Finally, the best kinds of goals are timely, in that they can be achieved within the near future. You may have a long-term goal of becoming an engineer, which is great. However, you may want to set a goal such as, "I will enter my project into the science fair," so that you can experience a sense of achievement in the short term.

Now, take a look at what you have learned about explaining yourself and understanding your strengths and come up with one or two SMART goals. They can be things like, "I want to write a note to my teacher, with my parents' help, to explain how I can best participate in class discussions this semester," or "I want to work on explaining why loud noises bother me in the cafeteria so I can convince my friends to eat in a quieter place." Record one or two of your goals on a separate sheet of paper. If you can't think of any, read on and come back to this chapter when you are ready.

Congratulations! You have completed your personal profile, and you can use your strengths while you try out some of the strategies in this book related to working with teachers and completing

your work, getting along with other kids, understanding bullying, using social media and electronic communication, developing
healthy habits, handling emotions, and gaining more independence.
Your strengths can help you find a comfortable place for yourself
in high school.

2

WORKING WITH TEACHERS AND COMPLETING WORK

You may find that you don't always understand what your teachers want from you. In the younger grades, teachers posted a list of rules on the wall. In high school, however, teachers often expect students to understand the rules of classroom behavior and their expectations about assignments without stating these rules directly. This chapter will help you better understand some of what your teachers are saying, and decipher what your high school teachers expect of you.

QUIZ YOURSELF!
HOW WELL DO YOU WORK WITH YOUR TEACHERS?

Okay, here's another quiz that's all about you. Answer the questions below to figure out how well you understand and work with your teachers.

1. When a teacher writes "see me" on a paper, I:
   a. Ignore it, because I don't read teachers' comments.

    b. Want to see the teacher but don't know how or when to do so.

    c. Speak to my teacher after class or e-mail my teacher to set up a time to see him or her.

2. When my teacher assigns a paper I don't understand, I:

    a. Put off writing the paper until the last minute.

    b. Try to remember what the teacher said in class.

    c. Meet with my teacher to understand how to complete the paper.

3. When I have a long-term assignment, I:

    a. Remember I have to do it the day before.

    b. Start it and then forget about it.

    c. Plan each step in my calendar so that I'm not saving it until the last minute.

4. When I have a very busy week filled with assignments and tests, I:

    a. Often wind up staying up late.

    b. Try to do a little bit each day.

    c. Schedule my week in advance and plan out each task.

5. When I have to study for a test, I:

    a. Don't really study—after all, how will the teacher know what I do to prepare for the test?

    b. Look over the material.

    c. Ask the teacher how to prepare and often make a study guide of topics on the test.

How to score yourself:

If you answered mostly "a": You may need to develop some strategies to understand how to work with teachers, how to do well in their classes, and how to prepare for tests, papers, and long-term assignments. Read on in the chapter to uncover some ideas that may help you.

If you answered mostly "b": You are starting to develop ways to work with your teachers, and you have some good strategies. Read the chapter to see if you come up with some new ideas or can improve your strategies to help you get your work done more efficiently and work better with your teachers.

If you answered mostly "c": You have some effective strategies to ask for help from teachers and to complete your assignments. This chapter may provide some additional ideas to help you better communicate with your teachers and work even more efficiently.

DEALING WITH NEW EXPECTATIONS

High school teachers often have different expectations of their students than teachers in middle school do. For example, many, though certainly not all, high school teachers expect that students can finish work on their own and schedule their own time to complete these assignments, even if the assignment involves many steps that students are expected to complete over several days or weeks. They also generally expect students to finish their work without reminders.

High school teachers often have different expectations of their students than teachers in middle school do.

Here are some common expectations of most high school teachers. Read each statement below and think about whether you meet that expectation or not.

Do I:

- Finish work on my own?
- Complete long-term assignments and study for tests without constant reminders or help breaking down the assignments?

- Understand the rules of honesty and how to avoid **plagiarism** (copying other people's ideas or work)?
- Act polite and attentive during class?
- Participate in class discussions while staying on topic and being respectful of other students?
- Accept positive as well as negative feedback about my work?
- Communicate politely and appropriately with my teachers?

Now, look at the list above. We will discuss strategies for fulfilling each type of common expectation teachers have of their students.

One way to better understand what your teachers expect of you is to consult the **syllabus,** or course outline and course expectations, that they hand out, usually at the beginning of the school year.

Sometimes, in addition to the syllabus or course outline, teachers also hand out assignment sheets on a weekly or less regular basis, but the course outlines are still helpful guides about what you need to do. Teachers may also post short- and long-term assignments on a school website, so you should be sure to understand how to access this website. Remember that you are responsible for checking your e-mail or web-based system (if your school has one) so you know about upcoming assignments and communication from teachers and your school.

COMPLETING ASSIGNMENTS INDEPENDENTLY

In middle school, teachers often help students break down longer assignments into smaller steps, and check in with students about their progress. In high school, however, your teachers may expect you to understand how to complete your work independently. To complete your work independently, you have to:

- Write down the due dates of upcoming assignments.

- Write down the smaller steps involved in an assignment. For example, writing a research paper involves: 1) finding the right sources, 2) reading your sources and taking notes on them, 3) writing an outline, 4) writing the paper, 5) revising and editing the paper, and 6) completing a bibliography with the sources you used.
- For each smaller step, write down and keep track of a due date using a calendar or assignment book. (See below for one example of how to do this.)
- If you run into problems, check in with your teacher and ask questions before the assignment is due.

Note that there are many steps involved in a research paper and that you need to start well in advance of the due date. Completing a research paper on time involves your developing deadlines in your assignment book for each smaller step involved in producing the final paper.

Here is an example of how one student scheduled his work to complete a paper on the construction of the Brooklyn Bridge:

Table 2.1

OCTOBER						
SUN	MON	TUES	WED	THURS	FRI	SAT
			1	2	3	4
			Receive assign-ment from the teacher.	Go to the library and find sources.		Start reading sources and tak-ing notes on note cards.

(continued)

Table 2.1 *(continued)*

OCTOBER						
SUN	MON	TUES	WED	THURS	FRI	SAT
5	6	7	8	9	10	11
Continue taking notes. Finish 10 note cards, each of which has a fact or opinion about the construction of the bridge. Make sure I write down where I read each fact or opinion. Write down my sources for my **bibliography**.			Continue taking notes. Finish 10 more note cards.	Meet with teacher and show her the note cards.	Use note cards to start writing an outline with the idea for each paragraph.	Start writing the paper using the outline.
12	13	14	15			
Finish writing the paper.	Revise the paper. Have a parent read it over for mistakes.		Paper due!			

Note that this student checked in with his teacher for help with writing his paper, and he also did not save his work for the last minute. If you need help breaking down a long-term assignment into smaller steps, you can use this example as a model or ask a teacher, parent, or librarian for help.

Choosing a Planning System

In high school, you will need a planning system to keep track of when your assignments are due. Though your school may have a web-based system that lists assignments, keep in mind that not every teacher uses this system. In addition, the web-based system will not help you break down long-term assignments into smaller steps, as in the example above. You will need to find a planning system that works for you.

You will need to find a planning system that works for you.

One type of planning system that you can use is a weekly or monthly calendar or planner. You can use it to mark down what you need to do each day and plan the time when you are going to complete each step involved in an assignment. Seeing your assignments listed for each day helps you put them in order and arrange your time so you can complete them. This type of planning system is especially important if you have other activities to plan around, such as sports practice or after-school clubs. Keep in mind that teachers in high school do not usually accept excuses for late assignments, and they do not expect that they will have to help you complete your work. They may also take off points or downgrade you for work you hand in late. Be sure to check each teacher's policy about late work. Here is an example of how one student used her weekly planner to keep track of her assignments:

Table 2.2

			MAY			
SUN	MON	TUES	WED	THURS	FRI	SAT
				22	23	24
				Write down final biology exam date, time, and location in my planner. Robotics club meeting.	Ask my biology teacher about the format for the final.	
25	26	27	28	29	30	31
Read chapter 1 of book for English class. Algebra worksheet.	Put together all my old biology tests. Write down Spanish vocab words on flashcards.	Review two out of six total biology tests to study for the final. Review Spanish flashcards.	Review the next two biology tests. Have my parents quiz me on the Spanish flashcards.	Spanish vocab quiz, 10:00 am, room 213. Robotics club meeting. Review the last two biology tests.	Ask my biology teacher any last questions I have.	

(continued)

Table 2.2 *(continued)*

JUNE						
SUN	MON	TUES	WED	THURS	FRI	SAT
I	2					
Read chapter 2 of book for English class. Review biology material I have not yet mastered and get a good night's sleep.	Take the biology final exam at 9:00 am in classroom 202.					

If you find it hard to remember to consult your planner, you can use a dry-erase board or wall calendar that helps you visualize what you need to do. Some students remember tasks better if they see them posted on their wall. If you tend to be a visual person, this type of planning system may work better for you than just keeping a paper planner that you have to remember to check. Use a large calendar or dry-erase board in an area you look at regularly, and try to use different colors for different subjects or tasks so that you will see them and remember them. Experiment with planning systems until you find one that works for you, and be sure to consult it and update it each day with the new tasks you need to do.

In order to keep track of school papers, you can use one large binder or an accordion folder that holds all of your papers. That way, you won't need to keep track of multiple folders—only one. If you use an accordion folder, you can label the part of the folder for each class. If you use a binder, you can use color-coded dividers to differentiate between classes.

Avoiding Plagiarism

One of the other common expectations of high school teachers is that the ideas you hand in on papers and other work are your own. The following are some guidelines for avoiding plagiarism, though you should be sure to check with each teacher about his or her policies regarding citing other people's words and ideas:

- You cannot copy work from another person, the internet, a book, or another source. The ideas you hand in should be your own, not those of a parent or tutor.
- If you are using information from a book, the internet, or another source, be sure to state where you got your information.
- You cannot copy directly from a book, the internet, or another source, unless you are quoting from that source and using quotation marks to indicate what you copied. You have to put ideas into your own words.
- If you quote directly from a book, the internet, or another source, be sure to put the information in quotes ("") and cite where you got it.
- If you have any questions about plagiarism, be sure to ask your teacher or your librarian.

Some students commit plagiarism without intending to, so if you are confused about how to use sources, be sure to ask your teacher well in advance of the final due date of your paper.

WHAT DO I DO IF ...

Question: I don't understand when I am plagiarizing other people's ideas. What do I do?
Answer: Speak to your English or history teacher or school librarian about what plagiarism is and how to avoid it. They can show you how to paraphrase (meaning put sources into your own words) and how to quote from and cite the sources you use to write papers or to complete other projects. Your school librarian can also help you keep track of the sources you use in a bibliography.

PARTICIPATING IN CLASSROOM DISCUSSIONS

Consider the following two students:

If you saw Alex in his history class, you would notice that he often wears a hood over his head, until his teacher asks him to put it down. He is usually slumped over his desk sleeping. When he does wake up, it's only long enough to contribute an off-topic remark to class discussion. Once, he was even caught texting on his phone. He thought his teacher wouldn't notice because he hid the phone under the desk, but she did and took his phone away for the class period. After all, who can blame him? He has no interest in American history. He is interested in rocketry, however, so he likes to speak about this subject when he can. He thinks history is a waste of time, as he has told his history teacher many times. He also tends to interrupt classmates and can be argumentative at times.

Now, consider Cameron. When he enters history class, he notes the homework assignment written on the board and writes it down in his planner. He then opens his notebook, ready for class discussion. His phone is turned off and stored in his backpack. He asks questions or contributes comments related to what the class is talking about. He sits straight in his chair and takes off his hat. Though he prefers math to history, he tries to find something interesting in what the class is studying. He waits until his classmates and teacher are finished speaking before he speaks, and he does not argue with his classmates or teacher.

Which of the following students is:

- Likely to receive a better grade for classroom behavior and participation?
- Likely to have the teacher say yes when he asks for help?
- Likely to be regarded well by the teacher and his classmates?

It's probably not a mystery that Cameron is likely to receive a better grade for classroom discussion, have the teacher be more willing to help him, and be better liked by his teacher and classmates. He is also likely to learn more and do better in the class by following these rules:

- He arrives in class ready to learn by removing his hat or hood and taking out his notebook.
- He puts his cell phone away during class, as most schools require, and turns it off so he is not tempted to use it.
- He writes down the assignment each day in his planner.
- He contributes related remarks to classroom discussions, even if he is not interested in the material.
- He sits up in his chair and does not slump, and his posture conveys or tells people that he is interested in learning.

- He does not interrupt his teacher or classmates or become argumentative.

Though each teacher has slightly different expectations, all teachers expect their students to be polite and attentive in class.

Maintaining Proper Body Language

In addition, teachers expect students to have the proper **body language,** or to convey the right things in the way they hold their body. Here are some guidelines for proper body language in the classroom:

- Stand or sit straight.
- If possible, look teachers in the eye when speaking to them. If this is uncomfortable for you, you may want to speak to your teacher about it and explain that you are not trying to be impolite but that looking people in the eye is difficult for you. This is part of explaining yourself to others, and it will help your teacher understand you better.
- Look at the person who is speaking.
- Do not wear hats or hoods in class.
- Do not cross your arms, as this gesture can be interpreted as unfriendly.
- Do not stare at your phone or use cell phones or mobile devices during conversations or class time.

You send many messages to teachers with the way you hold your body. If you are confused about what type of body language you should use in class, try to follow the points above to send a message to your teachers that you are interested in the class and ready to participate.

Speaking About Your Interests

You may have a lot of interests and areas that you find fascinating—whether they are languages, time periods in history, or areas of science. It's great to learn more about these interests, and there may be times when you will study them in school. At these times, it's completely acceptable for you to speak about your interests in class. However, at other times, you have to speak about the topic that you are studying in class. Though it can be hard, you are expected to speak about what the teacher wants to talk about—not your interests.

Make sure you are allowing others in the classroom time to speak as well. A good guideline to follow is to speak for less than a minute.

Also, make sure you are allowing others in the classroom time to speak as well. A good guideline to follow is to speak for less than a minute (unless you are giving a presentation). This gives other students time to contribute their ideas to the class discussion, too.

If you want to contribute to class discussion, ask yourself the following questions:

- "Is what I am speaking about on the topic or off the topic?"
- "Have I been speaking for longer than a minute?"
- "Am I responding to what my teacher and classmates are saying, or am I just contributing what I'm interested in?"

If you find that you need help controlling your interests, you can speak to your teacher about having a non-verbal sign, such as having the teacher touch his or her nose or shoulder, to indicate when you are off topic or not speaking about what the class needs to speak about.

COMMUNICATING WITH YOUR TEACHERS

Communicating with your teachers in high school can be tricky at times. Even if you don't particularly like a certain teacher, you may still need to ask that teacher for help, respond to his or her criticism without getting upset, write polite e-mails to that person, and have polite and effective conversations with the teacher. The section below will give you some suggestions about how to communicate with teachers in these types of situations.

Asking for Help

High school is full of unfamiliar situations, including new types of assignments and class work. These unfamiliar situations may at first make you uncomfortable, because you may worry about making a mistake. But the fact is, mistakes are one way to learn. As the revolutionary physicist Albert Einstein once said, "Anyone who has never made a mistake has never tried anything new."

Occasionally, you may find yourself confused about these new types of assignments or unable to complete your work without some help. Though you may feel uncomfortable asking for help because you don't want to show your teachers that you don't understand something, it is acceptable to ask for help. While it may seem that no one asks for help, the reality is that everyone needs help at some point! As Albert Einstein remarked in the quote above, making mistakes is part of learning—in fact, it's part of the process of scientific research too. If you don't make mistakes, you are likely not learning anything. While it is natural to want to hide your mistakes or pretend that you understand everything, the truth is that no one understands everything. There will come a point when you don't understand something, whether it is material you are studying or how to complete an assignment, and you need to ask your teacher for help.

Making mistakes is part of learning. If you don't make mistakes, you are likely not learning anything.

There are ways to ask for help that are better than other ways because they are polite and make the person giving the help feel more willing to do so. Consider the following conversation between a student named Ella and her teacher:

> **ELLA:** Hey, that assignment you gave was really annoying! Does it have to be due tomorrow? I mean, I know you gave it to us two weeks ago, but I had a lot more important things to do, like going to some really good concerts. Anyway, could you meet with me today? I mean, I need help!

Whoa. It seems like Ella has made a few critical errors in asking for help. Can you name them?

You might have noticed that she insults the teacher by calling the assignment annoying, which does not make her teacher feel excited about helping her. She has saved the assignment for the last minute because she was going to concerts (an excuse the teacher isn't likely to accept for handing in work late), and now, Ella wants help right away. She isn't being considerate about the teacher's schedule, and the teacher may have other things to do.

> **ELLA:** Hi, Ms. Brown. Is it okay if I speak to you about the project now?
>
> **MS. BROWN:** Yes, now is a good time for us to speak.
>
> **ELLA:** Thank you very much. After you gave out the assignment yesterday, I read it over, and I'm confused about a few things. I tried to start the research on my own, and I wanted to show you what I've done. I know the project isn't due for another two weeks, but I wanted to get started on it and make sure I'm on the right track.

What has Ella done better here? First, she asked the teacher if it was a good time to speak. She also started on the project right after it was assigned, giving her plenty of time to clarify questions or problems with the teacher. She also started doing the work on her own, so she could show the teacher that she was trying to do the work before asking for help. Teachers are often more likely to provide help if they know that you have started the project on your own. Most importantly, Ella was polite and considerate throughout her conversation.

While Ella was fortunate enough to be able to press the "restart" button, you don't always get that opportunity in real life. Instead, make sure you approach your teachers the first time with a polite attitude—and well in advance of deadlines. You may feel nervous at first about asking for help, but most teachers are very willing to help you if you ask them politely and not when they are busy.

Handling Criticism

Another subject related to asking for help is handling criticism. Let's return to Ella. She is now receiving feedback on a history paper that was full of factual errors and grammatical mistakes. Here's her response to her teacher:

> ELLA: Well, you gave me a really low grade on this paper. That sucks. I need this good grade to get into college. Can you change my grade? I guess you don't care about that. Who cares about the paper topic anyway? I don't want to be a historian or anything. I know you gave us an assignment sheet that said we need to hand in a factually correct paper with good grammar, but I lost that sheet. It's not my fault my paper was bad.

Wow. Ella is really not on the right track here. Can you spot what she's doing wrong? First, she does not accept responsibility for her poor grade, though the teacher clearly explained in advance that students need to turn in factually and grammatically accurate papers. In addition, she again insults the teacher and says that the paper is not important. Finally, she expects the teacher to change the grade, which most teachers are unwilling to do unless they have calculated your grade incorrectly (such as by accidentally marking correct answers as incorrect). In general, students should never ask teachers to change grades. That's why it's important to ask teachers for help *before* you hand in an assignment; after you hand it in, there is usually nothing a teacher can do to help you. Sometimes, teachers offer students the opportunity to rewrite or redo an assignment, but these types of opportunities are not provided as often in high school as they may have been in middle school. Instead, teachers expect you to follow directions and get the assignment right the first time you complete a paper or project.

Let's push the "restart" button again and see Ella approach her teacher in the right way.

> **ELLA:** Hi, Ms. Brown. I tried to follow your instructions for writing the paper, but I guess I really didn't get them. Can we meet when it's convenient for you, so I can understand how to do better on the next paper?

Ella has done much better this time around. Most importantly, she accepts responsibility for her poor work, and she asks the teacher for help to understand what she did wrong so that she can improve on the next paper. She uses the meeting with the teacher *not* as an opportunity to complain, but instead as a chance to learn from her mistakes. Though accepting feedback can be hard, it will help Ella improve.

Writing Emails to Teachers and Other Adults

When you write an e-mail or text message, you should first consider who your audience or the recipient of the message is. For example, if you write an e-mail to a teacher or other adult, you need to be more polite and formal (meaning using full sentences and correct wording) than if you were writing to a friend.

Here are the rules about writing an e-mail (or text) to a teacher or another adult who is not your parent:

- Address the teacher using his or her title, such as "Ms.," "Mrs.," "Mr.," or "Dr.," and his or her last name. If you are confused about which title the teacher uses, consult handouts the teacher has given you, which are likely to have his or her title and name on them.

- Do not start your e-mail with informal greetings that you would use with friends, such as "hey," or "hi."
- State your question or request clearly, such as "I would like to meet with you to talk about my research paper," so that the teacher understands what you want.
- Do not make unreasonable demands or requests, such as "I need to meet with you today," (as the teacher may be busy), or "I want you to show me how to do the research paper." Keep in mind that while most teachers are willing to help you, they have busy schedules, have to help a lot of students, and will not do the work for you.
- Keep in mind that if your school has an e-mail system, you are responsible for checking your school e-mail so that you can respond to e-mails from teachers and other adults at school. When the teacher e-mails you, be sure to e-mail him or her back soon afterward.
- When writing to adults, avoid using e-mail or text abbreviations that you would use with your friends, such as "Lol" or "2mrw." These types of abbreviations are too informal for communication with adults.
- Always end the e-mail by thanking the teacher.
- Follow these rules if you are writing to any adults, not just teachers.

Consider the following two examples of e-mails to teachers. Who did a better job of writing the e-mail in a way that will get a good response?

Hey,

I need to meet. Will meet at classroom 2mrw. Or else I won't do the paper. j

Dear Ms. Smith,

    I am writing to ask for help on the paper. What time would work for you? I am free today or tomorrow at 3. Thank you for your time.

It's pretty clear that the second e-mail is better, more polite, and far more effective. The writer addresses the teacher by her title and last name and then states exactly what he wants, while the first writer starts with the informal "hey" (not the way to address teachers or other adults) and does not state what he wants. In addition, the first writer uses abbreviations and makes unreasonable requests (such as asking to meet right away). Keep in mind that teachers don't understand or like text and e-mail abbreviations such as "2mrw," (tomorrow) or "j" (joking), so it's better not to use them. Finally, the second e-mail thanks the teacher, which is a necessary part of writing an e-mail in which you ask for a favor or for help. People are more likely to help you if you thank them in advance and keep your **tone** (the way your e-mail sounds) polite. The tone of your e-mail is established by addressing the recipient correctly, using formal language, and thanking the person.

Having Conversations With Adults

Conversations with adults, like emails to adults, often have a different tone than the conversations you have with kids your age. The tone of music refers to whether it is loud or soft, fast-paced or slow. The **tone** of a conversation refers to how your words sound to other people. Tone is just as important as the words you say.

The tone of a conversation is just as important as the words you say.

Some conversations have an angry tone, and some have a friendly tone. How do you know what type of tone a conversation has and how you contribute to the tone of the conversation? Here are clues to listen to in order to figure out the tone of a conversation:

- Is it loud or soft? Usually, a louder conversation means the people are excited or angry.
- Are the people speaking quickly or slowly? When people get excited, they speed up their words and speak more quickly.
- Are the people gesturing a lot? If so, they could be upset or excited.

When you have a conversation with an adult, such as a teacher, your tone should be different than when you speak with a person your own age or younger. For example, you should start off the conversation by setting a pleasant tone and greeting the other person by saying, "good morning," "hello," or "excuse me." You should look the other person in the eye and try to make your voice even and not too loud or soft, even if you are upset. Your tone is important because it is part of what you convey or communicate to other people. If, for example, you want to get help from someone, you want to approach that person with a friendly tone. If you feel as though people don't understand what you say, even though your words are generally polite, it could be because of the tone you are using. If you have trouble understanding your tone, or how you sound to other people, you should ask a trusted adult or friend to let you know how you sound.

In addition, no matter who you are speaking to, you want to be careful about your **body language,** or the way in which you hold your body. In general, when speaking to someone, you want to do the following:

- Look someone directly in the eye at least some of the time. It's okay to take breaks to look away, but you don't want to stare at the floor or behind the person for the entire conversation.

- Nod your head up and down if you agree with the person.
- Try not to cross your arms, as this gesture can be seen as unfriendly or hostile.
- Try not to tap your foot, sigh, or look at your watch, as these gestures can seem like you are impatient.
- During a conversation, do not send text messages or e-mails or look at your phone. While you may feel tempted to do so, these gestures are not considered friendly.

If you wonder how you sound or look to others while having a conversation, ask a trusted friend or adult. Your friend may let you know that some of the ways in which you hold your body or speak to others could be interpreted as unfriendly, even though you don't intend them to be. For example, you may feel more comfortable not looking people in the eye, but people may misinterpret this

WHAT DO I DO IF ...

Question: I try to act polite, but people, including kids and adults, often tell me I seem rude. What do I do?

Answer: While you may be trying to seem polite, keep in mind that there are lots of parts to a conversation. Part of it is the words you use, and the other parts of a conversation are how you speak and your body language. In order to have a polite conversation, you also have to think about your tone and your body language. Are you speaking in a soft, not-too-fast way, and are you looking other people in the eye? These are strategies that convey to other people that you are listening and being polite. Remember to try to answer their questions, and don't end the conversation abruptly if they aren't finished yet. Instead, wait until they are finished, and if you aren't sure, you can always say something like, "Is there anything else?" before ending the conversation. Also, be sure to say goodbye while looking at the other person.

behavior as unfriendly, even if you are only looking away because you are shy. Your friend may also let you know that you are doing a good job communicating with others in many ways, including the ways in which you hold your body and the tone you use. When you are speaking to others, try to think a bit about your tone and body language and how others might be interpreting these unspoken parts of the conversation.

A NOTE ABOUT GYM TEACHERS

Gym or P.E. teachers tend to have different expectations for their classes than other teachers, and they run their classes in different ways. As you know, much of gym class consists of playing games and sports. If you have trouble following the games or participating in them, you may want to approach your gym teacher for a conversation. If you need help thinking about how to approach the teacher, you can speak with your guidance counselor or parent first. This person can coach you about how to approach the teacher and give you an idea of what you might say.

If you speak to the gym teacher, he or she can help you by breaking down each step you need to follow in order to get ready for gym class, participate in the game, and get ready for the next class. In this discussion, you may or may not want to tell the gym teacher you have Asperger's (see the introduction of this book for a discussion about whether or not to reveal you have Asperger's to other people), but you may want to explain that you have difficulty following the game (if you do) or that you have **fine or gross motor issues**. If possible, bring documentation from your doctor to back up what you are saying, and consider meeting with your teacher or an administrator such as a principal with another teacher or a parent present.

You may decide that you can participate in gym class, or there may be another option for you, such as lifting weights or taking yoga. Be sure to follow your school's rules about which types of options are acceptable for gym class.

In order to be part of a team (if you don't want to play on the team), consider a position such as team manager or statistician. That way, you can participate in school events without playing on the team. Of course, if you want to play on the team, go ahead! You can also join club, intramural, or community sports teams or take up an activity such as swimming for fitness, club sports, hiking, horseback riding, surfing, golf, or skating.

SETTING GOALS

Now, it's time to set some personal goals about relating to teachers, as you might when starting a video game. In order to be attainable, goals have to be SMART in nature; that is, they must be:

Specific,
Measurable,
Attainable,
Realistic, and
Timely.

Look back to what you have learned about how to work with teachers, and try to establish two or three SMART goals. They can be goals like, "I will ask my math teacher for help three days before the next test," or "I will ask my teacher to let me know if I'm getting off track in a class discussion," or "I will begin to keep a planner and write down my nightly work and long-term assignments." Record one or two of your goals on a separate sheet of paper.

While it may seem confusing at first to know how to ask for help from high school teachers and how to convey that you are interested in their class, you can use the strategies in the chapter you just read to help you work well with your teachers.

3

GETTING ALONG
WITH OTHER KIDS
IN HIGH SCHOOL

High school offers you the chance to interact with a lot of different kids. You will have different classes for each subject and the opportunity to join after-school clubs and activities. It may be difficult at first to know how to get along with and connect with so many different kids. This chapter will present you with some strategies to relate to other kids in ways that help you make yourself understood and that allow you to connect with kids who share your interests.

QUIZ YOURSELF!
HOW WELL DO YOU GET ALONG WITH PEERS?

Here is another quiz about yourself. This time, you will answer questions about how well you relate to friends and classmates (or peers, people your own age) at school.

1. When I am talking to someone at school, I:
   a. Don't really notice what the other person is doing with his or her body or eyes.

    b. Try to notice if he or she is tapping a foot, which means he or she may be impatient.

    c. Try to notice a lot of different cues that come from his or her body language, including rolling eyes, tapping feet, looking at watches or the clock, and so on.

2. When I enter a classroom, I:

    a. Usually am not paying attention to what's going on in the room.

    b. Start removing my notebook from my backpack.

    c. Look around to figure out if there is a conversation already going on and if class has started yet.

3. When I work on group projects, I:

    a. Just do my own thing.

    b. Break up the work so each person does a part of the assignment on his or her own.

    c. Try to do my part of the work and support my classmates if they are having trouble completing their work.

4. When I want to hang out with someone or ask another person out on a date, I:

    a. Just hang around him or her until I hear about something going on.

    b. Send the person a text.

    c. Call the person or speak to him or her.

5. To connect with people I like at school, I:

    a. Play online games with other kids.

    b. Post some messages on social networks and check out other kids' pages to see what they are doing.

    c. Join clubs or teams that I like.

How to score yourself:

If you answered mostly "a": You may be isolating yourself from kids at school by over-connecting with technology or your thoughts and not connecting enough with people. While there's nothing wrong with video games or social networks or thinking about what you are interested in, read on in this chapter to find other opportunities to connect with people you may have something in common with at school.

If you answered mostly "b": You are looking around and figuring out how to work with and socialize with kids at school—and that's good. By reading this chapter, you may get additional ideas about how to find people at school whose company you would enjoy and how to work well with other students.

If you answered mostly "c": You are connecting with friends at school and with classmates, and that's great. Read on to find other ways that may be helpful to find people you will enjoy spending time with at school.

MAKING CONVERSATION

In high school, you will have the chance to meet and talk to a lot of different kids. It can be hard to know what to say, but making conversation is an important way to relate to other kids at school and find other kids you connect with. Read on to learn about some ways to start and continue conversations with other kids, and to decode non-verbal cues to help you understand what other kids are saying.

Body Language

While you may understand most of the words the kids at school say, you may not realize that a lot of their message comes from their body language—how they hold and use their body when they are talking to you or other kids. Body language isn't that hard to understand if you think about it as a code. Much like a symbol in a code stands for something else, each type of gesture and the way people hold their head or other parts of their body means something. Here are some common body gestures and postures (nothing obscene) and what they mean:

Crossed arms: This may mean a person is angry or defensive (meaning he or she is trying to protect him or herself). An added clue is that an angry person will also sometimes raise his or her voice, speak quickly, or start to flush or turn red in the face.

Tapping a foot: A person tapping his or her foot is often in a hurry or impatient.

Turning one's head to one side: This could mean a person is confused about what you are saying or is listening to you carefully.

Narrowing one's eyes: When a person narrows his or her eyes, he or she could be expressing doubt or distrust about what you are saying.

Winking: Winking could mean a person is in agreement with what you are saying or is just being friendly.

Nodding: A person nodding his or her head up and down usually means he or she is in agreement with what you are saying. A person shaking his or her head side to side is saying no or disagreeing with what you are saying.

Observe your teachers, friends, parents, or other people. Note their body language and try to decode it, or figure out what it means.

Now, it's your turn to break the code of body language and gestures. Observe your teachers, friends, parents, or other people. Note their body language and try to decode it, or figure out what it means. If they are speaking, be sure to note the words they are using, as well. You can practice by asking friends to make faces showing a type of emotion and then practice guessing what it means. You might be surprised at how quickly you learn to identify emotions in people's bodies and faces by acting like a code-breaker. Sometimes, it may be hard to figure out the code, and, if so, you may have to ask people directly what they mean.

Conversation Starters

When kids are hanging out during lunch or after school, here are some of the common topics of conversation they may bring up:

- Their opinions about classes, teachers, or homework.
- The movies or TV shows they watch.
- The video games they play.
- The music they listen to.
- Other interests they have: playing sports, watching sports, making art, reading, manga, taking photographs, etc.
- Their plans for their weekend or vacations.

A lot of conversations among kids have to do with very little, in actuality. They simply like to hang out and make jokes. If you are wondering how to start a conversation with other kids, you may want to try one of the "conversation starters" below. These are like keys that are inserted into the engine of the conversation to make it go. After that, the conversation can often go more smoothly:

- "Do you like the class we have together?"
- "What did you think about our homework or last test?"
- "What video games do you play?"
- "Which teams do you follow?"
- "Did you see the game on TV?"
- "What kind of music do you like?"
- "What's your favorite game on your phone?"
- "What bands have you been listening to lately?"

These are some really basic ideas. A conversation starter should be:

- Something that is not insulting or rude to the person you are speaking with or to other people.
- A comment that can open up the other person and welcome him or her to contribute ideas.
- A way to share information rather than a one-sided conversation in which only you participate.

After beginning a conversation, be sure to listen to the other person and follow up on his or her ideas. A conversation is kind of like a long drive with another person. After inserting the key into the engine of conversation, you want to make sure that you take turns driving the conversation. That is, allow the other person time to "take the wheel" and contribute thoughts and ideas, just like you would take turns driving during a road trip. A conversation does not always have to be shared exactly fifty-fifty, but what makes a conversation "go" is the ability of both participants (or, in the case of group conversations, all participants) to contribute.

When you don't know what to say, you can always say something like, "Wow, I like your ideas" or "That's really cool!" Complimenting another person is a really good way to keep the conversation moving and to become better friends with someone.

Complimenting another person is a really good way to keep the conversation moving and to become better friends with someone.

What other conversation starters have you tried that you think are successful?

The good thing about these "keys to conversation" is that they can be used in any place—whether you are waiting for class to start, at lunch, or at a party or any other place hanging out with other kids.

Now, think about the following "keys to conversation." How well do think the following conversation starters will work?

- "Don't you hate [a specific kid or teacher]?"
- "Don't you hate [a class or activity]?"
- "Wasn't that class awful?"
- "You say some weird things in class."

These are just some examples, but you should guess that some of these keys may not be good ways to start the engine of conversation. While it's true that kids often make jokes and say rude things about other kids or teachers, you have to know your audience before launching into such a conversation. If you don't know how the person you are speaking to will react to that kind of comment, it's best not to start that way. During the course of the conversation, you may get a better sense of how the other person thinks, and then you can judge whether you think these kinds of statements are appropriate. It's never a good idea to start a conversation with a comment that is insulting to the other person. You can voice your opinion about the other person's ideas, but you want to do so in a way that is not insulting, such as, "I don't always agree with what you say in English class, but I want to hear more of your ideas." Also, you may want to bring up these types of opinions later in the conversation, as they often do more to shut down than to start conversations.

Bumps in the Conversational Road

Bumps in the conversational road are comments or other things that can make a conversation get detoured or make it end altogether. Just as there are bumps in the road that make a car slow down or stop, there are words or phrases that result in interrupting or stopping a conversation. The following types of comments can cause a bump or disruption in the conversation:

- "What you are saying is stupid."
- "You are really dumb."
- "You don't know what you are talking about."
- "Let me talk."
- "I need to interrupt you."
- "I don't really care about what you are saying."

Changing the conversation topic abruptly, not listening to the other person, or only wanting to talk about your own interests can also cause a detour or end to the conversation. While the conversation is going, do your best to listen to the other person, be polite and receptive to his or her ideas (even if you do not agree with them), and let the other person contribute.

Personal Space

Some people reach out and physically touch other people during conversation. They will, for example, touch the other person's arm or shoulder or pat the other person's leg. In general, however, it is better not to touch others unless you are very good friends, as they may misinterpret what you are doing and think it means you want to date them or have closer contact with them, even if you do not intend to convey this message. You should try to put about an arm's length between yourself and the other person you are speaking to, especially if the other person is someone you don't know very well or an adult. People usually like to have a bit of personal space around them, unless they are speaking to a very close friend, parent or other relative, or a boyfriend or girlfriend.

Keep about an arm's length between yourself and other people, particularly adults and people you don't know as well, during conversations.

WORKING ON GROUP PROJECTS

You will use the strategies related to how to speak with peers and friends in different situations in high school. For example, you may be expected to work with other students on group projects or discussions instead of just completing the work on your own.

Group work can be difficult. Your group has to figure out how you are going to divide up the work, and you may find that you disagree with your group members. Disagreements can be part of the process; it's all right to disagree politely if the group can then work through these issues and come up with a solution. Even though you may disagree with others in your group, you are still responsible for the following:

- Doing the work required of you.
- Figuring out how to help your group, at the very least by doing some part of the work.
- Figuring out a compromise if you disagree with your group members.
- Taking part in in-class, after-school, and other work sessions.
- Contributing to the final presentation or project.

Consider the way in which Sam, a high school sophomore, takes part in group work.

Sam was assigned to a group of four students in his English class to work on a presentation on the book the class was reading. Sam had not read most of the book, but he was sure that his group members were wrong about their interpretation of the book. He disagreed with them during their in-class group planning sessions, and he did not join their after-school work sessions or respond to their e-mails. In the end, his group finished most of the work without him, and Sam did not take an active role in presenting the work in class. As a result, he received a low grade.

If you were one of Sam's group members, would you have liked participating in his group?

Let's consider what Sam did wrong. Did you notice any of these mistakes?:

- He did not do the required work beforehand, as he did not read the book his group was presenting about.
- He spent his time disagreeing with the group rather than trying to work with them.
- He did not join the group's in-class, after-school, or e-mail work sessions.
- He did not join in the group presentation.

Now, consider what happened the next time Sam participated in a group project:

Sam was supposed to take part in his group's presentation about the book they were reading in English class. Before their work began, Sam finished the reading, and he came to their work sessions with ideas about how to do the presentation. His group members had different ideas, so the group spoke to their teacher, who said they could present both ideas. Sam also joined his group in after-school work sessions and responded to their e-mails. Finally, on the day of the presentation, Sam and each of the group members took part in the final presentation, as they had all agreed in advance about which role they would take in the presentation. The presentation was successful, and Sam and his group members received a high grade on it.

You should note that Sam was much more successful this time around. Here is what he did right:

- He did the required work beforehand.
- He came to the group with ideas.
- He and his group consulted their teacher when they had a disagreement.
- Sam participated fully in in-class and after-school work sessions, and he responded to his team members' emails.
- Sam took part in the final presentation.

Working well with a group involves recognizing and appreciating other people's needs and concerns. These skills are also involved in developing friendships with other kids.

DEVELOPING FRIENDSHIPS

In high school, you may have to find new friends and develop new friendships in different ways than you did in middle school. You may have started a new, larger school. You may still go to school with people you knew in middle school, but you may want to develop new friendships in high school. In middle school, you may have just made friends with kids who were in your classes. While you may find friends in your classes in high school, you may also want to join after-school clubs, sports, and other activities to form new friendships.

Tips for Finding New Friends

Here are some ideas for broadening your group of friends or for finding new friends in high school:

- Join after-school or community activities that you enjoy, including sports teams, clubs, or other groups. Your local library may also have groups you can join, such as book clubs.

- If you can't figure out which clubs or activities to join, speak with a teacher or advisor at your school who may be able to recommend an activity related to your interests. For example, if you enjoy reading plays, you may want to join the drama club, either as an actor or as part of the tech crew. If you like math, the math club or physics club might be right for you. Look at a recent yearbook in the school library or a list of current clubs to get a sense of what the possible clubs and activities are.
- If you like playing video games, consider joining a gaming club so that you can talk about and play games with other kids.
- If you can't find any groups to join, it's okay. You can connect to other kids through common interests outside of school, such as playing video games or Dungeons and Dragons or talking about *The Lord of the Rings*. The important thing is not to always hang out or play games on your own, but to find other people in your class who like doing the same things you do.
- Try to find friends who have lunch at the same time you do so that you can have someone to sit with during lunch periods.
- Find out if your school offers student mentoring or tutoring programs. These programs can be a great way to become friendly with another student, perhaps an older one who can give you some helpful, tried-and-true advice about how to do well in school and how to handle different kinds of social activities and issues at school.

It's all right to make friends with people who share some, even if not all, of your interests. For example, if you are interested in music, you may find kids in band who can speak about music with you, even if they don't share your other interests. If you feel that you do not have much in common with kids at your school, try branching out. Join activities or clubs online (with your parents' permission) or in your community to find other people who have similar interests to yours.

WHAT DO I DO IF ...

Question: I want to be friends with other kids, but I'm not interested in what they're interested in, and I don't keep up with current music and fashion. What do I do?

Answer: You may be able to find friends with similar interests by joining clubs, such as robotics, math, physics, book clubs, or gaming clubs. With your parents' permission, you can also join Asperger's websites and chat rooms (see the "Resources" section at the end of this book). Finally, if you are interested in learning more about current music and clothes, ask a friend who's up-to-date in these areas to share some current music with you and to take you shopping.

Video Games and Your Social Life

Video games are great, and there is nothing wrong with playing them. However, like everything else, they deserve to be enjoyed in moderation. If you are playing them during all your free time, you may not be spending enough time on school work, sleep, or hanging out with friends. Instead of playing alone (or with friends online), try to invite friends over so they can play with you. You can also join a gaming club as another way to share your interests with other kids at school. Keep in mind that the virtual world is not the actual world, and playing video games is not the same as interacting with people in real life. If you are playing so many hours of video games that you aren't sleeping, eating, doing your schoolwork, or spending time with friends and family, you should speak to a trusted adult, such as a parent or teacher. Usually, it's not necessary to totally disconnect from games, but you need to spend time doing other things for your health, well-being, and school performance. If you have any concerns about your gaming, visit On-line Gamers Anonymous at http://www.olganon.org. They run a self-help support group to help people who have become so addicted to gaming that it interferes with their lives and their ability to enjoy anything else.

Cliques

Just like in middle school, high school students are often divided into **cliques,** or social groups, though sometimes, high school students are more willing to socialize with people outside their immediate social groups than middle school students are. Some common types of social groups in high school include the "jocks," or athletes, and the kids who participate in drama. There are other kinds of cliques as well. While it may be hard to break into a new clique, one strategy you may try is to make friends with one of the kids in a social group and to have that person introduce you to his or her friends. For example, if your neighbor is in a different group, you can try to hang out with that person in the neighborhood and then

WHAT DO I DO IF ...

Question: I want to hang out with friends, but I find it really exhausting—all that talking. What do I do?

Answer: It's understandable if you find it really tiring to hang out with friends, especially those who talk a lot. People expect a little bit of talking when they meet, but you can try getting together for activities where you won't have to talk the entire time, like watching a movie or playing a video game. You could also try to meet up with friends for limited amounts of time, such as lunch.

meet other people through your friend. Remember that it's never a good idea to be friends with people who are mean to you or who make you feel negative about yourself.

DATING

Dating can be a part of high school social life. If you are not ready to date, it's okay—take your time and don't be pressured into it just because other people are doing it. It's fine to start dating when you're ready, and for many people, that means not dating until you are in college or finish high school. However, if you feel that you are interested in asking someone out, it can be hard to figure out how to do so. You may want to read a book that helps you understand dating such as *The Teen Survival Guide to Dating & Relating: Real-World Advice for Teens on Guys, Girls, Growing Up, and Getting Along* by Annie Fox. The author of this book helps you think about what you want in your relationships with other people and the importance of respecting yourself. The book also helps people who are thinking about their sexual identity, meaning whether they like people of the same or opposite sex (or both) and how they think about themselves.

Here are some issues to keep in mind if you are thinking about asking someone on a date or accepting another person's invitation for a date:

- Don't do anything that makes you feel uncomfortable, and tell the other person if you feel uncomfortable.
- Don't ask the other person to do anything that makes him or her feel uncomfortable, and listen to what the other person says.
- Do not touch the other person unless he or she is agreeable to it, meaning he or she conveys that it is okay through words or physical gestures.

- When you are asking someone out or going out with another person, it is never all right for that person to threaten or hurt you or to ask you to stop seeing your other friends. If you have concerns about your relationships and whether they are safe and healthy, be sure to consult a trusted adult.

It's difficult to get up the courage to ask someone else out, and it's understandable if you feel nervous about doing so. Here are some ideas to make asking someone else out a bit easier:

- Try to join a club or activity where you meet people you like. If you are doing an activity with a person you like, whether it's Dungeons and Dragons, theater, or yoga, it may be more natural to ask that person to hang out together after your activity or at some other time.
- If you have a friend in common, you can ask the friend to ask the person you are interested in to hang out with you (and perhaps, at first, you can also hang out with the person you are interested in along with your mutual friend).
- It's better to ask someone out in person or on the phone. Asking by text or e-mail might be easier, but the person might not think you are serious if you don't ask in person.
- Don't feel like you have to ask right away. Instead, get to know someone first. Ask someone out when the person is alone and not busy doing something else.
- Keep in mind that just because someone is friendly to you, it may not mean that the person wants to date you. The other person may just be interested in being friends. If you are wondering what the other person has in mind, try asking a friend you trust who also knows the other person. That person may be able to provide you with more information about the intentions of the person you are interested in.

- If you are turned down or rejected, it can be painful. Try to keep in mind that there are other people out there, and it may just take a bit of time to find the right one.

Keep in mind that just because someone is friendly to you, it may not mean that the person wants to date you.

It might be easier to see someone else ask a person out on date than to do so yourself, so consider what Elizabeth does below to ask out Jake, a guy who's in her math class. By the way, it's okay for girls to ask out guys, and it's okay for girls to ask out girls and guys to ask out guys. For more about questions of **sexual identity,** meaning your ideas about yourself and how you think you should behave based on whether you are a guy or girl, see *GLBTQ: The Survival Guide for Gay, Lesbian, Bisexual, Transgender, and Questioning Teens* by Kelly Huegel.

Elizabeth finds Jake waiting for math class with a lot of other people around:

ELIZABETH: Oh, hey, Jake. I don't know if you'd like to do this, but do you want to go out? I mean, I have a car, and we can drive to the movies. What do you think?

Elizabeth is no doubt nervous, but let's think about a way she might have approached this situation differently. She asked Jake out when he was around a lot of other people, so he might feel on the spot or embarrassed, even if he does want to go out with Elizabeth.

Also, she immediately puts herself down by saying he might not want to go out with her—that's not necessary. Elizabeth should project a feeling of realistic confidence (but not boasting) rather than putting herself down. She also makes it sound like she is desperate by telling Jake that she has a car, making it seem like her car is the reason he might date her. Finally, she puts Jake on the spot and asks him to respond immediately.

Now, let's think of a way Elizabeth could have made the whole situation easier for herself and spared herself some embarrassment if the situation did not work out the way she wanted.

> Elizabeth finds Jake alone working on his math homework in the library.
>
> **ELIZABETH:** Oh, hey, Jake.
> **JAKE:** Hey, Elizabeth.
> **ELIZABETH:** Are you working on tonight's math homework?
> **JAKE:** Yeah, I just started.
> **ELIZABETH:** Oh, do you mind if I sit down and do the math homework too?
> **JAKE:** Sure, no problem.

At this point, Elizabeth and Jake can start working together on math, and their conversation will more natural. Elizabeth can bring up a subject that they have in common. Making conversation about another subject can also help Elizabeth feel less nervous when she asks Jake if he's interested in going out with her.

> **ELIZABETH:** Hey, do you know that our English teacher, Ms. O'Connor, said we have to see the school play this weekend?
> **JAKE:** Oh, yeah, that's right.

ELIZABETH: I was going to go on Friday. Do you know when you are going to go?

JAKE: I think I can go on Friday too. See you there, and save me a seat if you get there first.

ELIZABETH: Okay! See you then.

Though you never know exactly how a conversation will go ahead of time, Elizabeth does several things right this time around, and she makes the whole dating thing a lot easier on herself. Do you notice what she did?

- First, she found Jake alone, at a time when they could speak privately and without being embarrassed by being around others.
- She started talking to Jake about some of the things they had in common, such as their math homework and the play they had to see for English class. She was able to calm her nerves a bit by speaking about the math homework before asking if Jake was going to the play.
- Elizabeth and Jake started working on their math homework together, making their conversation more natural. That way, when the play came up, it seemed like part of the flow of conversation and less likely to put Jake on the spot.
- Elizabeth said she was going to the play and asked Jake when he was going to attend, making Jake feel less pressured into the date. Also, if Jake couldn't make it when she could, she would feel less embarrassed because she hadn't actually asked him out. If he had said he could not go when she could, she could either ask him to do something else or wait for another opportunity to ask him out.

Keep in mind that the hard thing about asking someone out for a date is that you never completely know what the person will

WHAT DO I DO IF ...

Question: I like a lot of girls and want to date them, but I find it really hard to tell if they are really interested in me or not. What do I do?

Answer: Dating can be a confusing situation for everyone, and it's hard to tell if someone likes you as a friend or as more than a friend, meaning as a girlfriend or boyfriend. Just because a girl is friendly or nice to you, it may not mean that she wants to date you. If you wonder whether she wants to date you, you can try to ask her to do something with you that doesn't necessarily seem like a date, like hanging out after school or just talking on the phone. If it seems to be going well, you might ask her out for something more date-like, such as going to a movie or a party. Try to ask the girl out when you are alone so you and she can have privacy and not feel embarrassed. If you are really in doubt about what to do, talk to a trusted friend who can keep your secret that you like another person.

---

say ahead of time. In other words, there is no way to control the whole situation, unlike, say, a video game you know well or a book you've read before. But that's also what makes relationships with people more interesting—they are sometimes unpredictable and can be surprising in good ways. However, timing is really important. You are more likely to be successful if you find a time to speak to someone when you are comfortable, alone, and having a natural conversation about shared interests.

You can get better at carrying on conversations, asking people to hang out, and even at dating by practicing. If you don't have opportunities to practice, you can always have a mock or pretend conversation with a trusted adult or friend. Try role-playing, or acting out different roles, for situations such as going to a party, calling a friend on the phone, or asking someone out. That way, you can come up with some good ideas about what to say ahead of time, before you are actually in those situations. The more you practice these types of situations, through role-playing and in reality, the better and more comfortable you will become at them. You can also ask a friend who has dated or who has an active social life what he or she does to get along with people and to ask them out. Keep in mind, though, that you don't have to do exactly what your friend does and that you can come up with your own style of socializing.

SETTING GOALS

Now, it's time to set some personal goals about relating to other kids in high school, as you might set goals when starting a video game. In order to be attainable, goals have to be SMART in nature; that is, they must be:

Specific,
Measurable,
Attainable,
Realistic, and
Timely.

Think about two or three goals you have about relating to other students or friends in high school. They can be things like, "I will join a club this semester to meet other kids interested in what I'm interested in," or "I will meet with my group members this week to work on our presentation together," or "I will try to start a conversation with the cute girl in my biology class before class starts." Write down one or two of your goals on a separate sheet of paper.

While high school may at first seem frightening if you are new to the school or if there are a lot of new kids, high school also presents the opportunity for you to improve your conversational skills and to learn to make new friends. In the process, you may discover new parts of yourself and improve your social skills, enabling you to feel more comfortable in new situations.

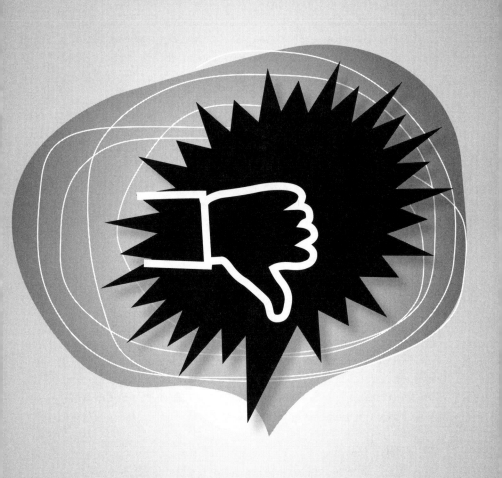

4

BULLYING

While high school offers you the chance to get to know—and hang out with—new kids, you may also encounter kids who aren't very good friends. Once in a while, you may find yourself interacting with a kid who intentionally wants to make you feel bad and who repeatedly does so through bullying. This chapter will help you recognize and deal with bullies.

QUIZ YOURSELF!
HOW WELL DO YOU UNDERSTAND BULLYING?

Answer the questions below to figure out if you can recognize and deal with bullies:

1. If another kid asks me to do something I find embarrassing, I:
   a. Do what the kid wants—after all, I need to make friends.
   b. Sit quietly and hope the kid stops asking.
   c. Tell the kid to stop, or ask a teacher to ask him to stop.

2. To me, the best friends are:
   a. Kids who want to sit with me at lunch, even if they say mean things.
   b. Kids who are nice and are in my classes.
   c. Kids who make me feel good about myself and accepted.
3. If I've asked a kid to stop making fun of me, but he or she won't, I:
   a. Try to avoid him or her.
   b. Tell him to stop again.
   c. Make sure I tell a teacher or trusted adult.
4. If a kid sends me threatening or harassing e-mails or text messages, I:
   a. Answer them back, possibly with an insult.
   b. Delete them immediately.
   c. Show them to my parents or another adult.
5. A person who asks me to do something dangerous is:
   a. A friend who likes to have fun.
   b. A person I have to put up with.
   c. Someone I should not be friends with.

How to score yourself:

If you answered mostly "a": You might be accepting behavior from other kids or adults that qualifies as bullying, as this behavior involves intentional and repeated attempts to make you feel bad about yourself and to gain power over you. You may need to report this behavior to an adult or teacher if it continues. Read this chapter to gain some ideas about how to handle bullying.

If you answered mostly "b": You don't want to accept behavior from other people that is cruel or bullying, which is good. You can use this chapter to develop strategies to help you deal with this behavior.

If you answered mostly "c": You are doing a good job recognizing and handling bullying behavior. This chapter may help you develop other ideas about how to handle bullying in high school.

WHAT IS BULLYING?

Bullying involves intentionally making someone else feel uncomfortable or unwanted, or attacking them physically, verbally, or through e-mail (or other forms of communication such as texts or posts on social networking sites). Bullying is often repeated, and it involves one person trying to gain power or control over another person. That is, a bully wants to feel more powerful than you and tell you what to do. Bullying can also include spreading rumors about another person. Remember that true friends never make you feel uncomfortable or ask you to do anything that you don't want to do.

Remember that true friends never make you feel uncomfortable or ask you to do anything that you don't want to do.

There are other things kids or adults can ask you to do that you may not initially recognize as bullying, but which involve bullying because the other person is forcing you to do something that you aren't comfortable with in an attempt to feel more powerful than you. Some of these bullying activities can include the following (though they are not limited to the following):

- Asking you to put yourself in physical harm, such as by climbing to an unsafe height or jumping from an unsafe height or entering an area that is off-limits or physically dangerous, such as an abandoned building, off-limits room at school, train track, road, etc.
- Asking you to harm another person or an animal or to damage a physical space.
- Asking you to send or give up personal information to another person or online, including your social security number, name, address, parents' information, etc.

- Forcing you to have contact with another person that is uncomfortable to you, whether it involves speaking to someone you do not know or touching someone in a way that is uncomfortable.
- Forcing you to give money or other valuables to someone or to bet on a situation, in the process risking your own money or valuables.

The common link between all of these activities is that the other person is forcing you to do something you find uncomfortable, physically or emotionally. You should not accept being placed in these situations, and you should never put another person in these situations, either. Note that each person can define what is uncomfortable for him or herself. Perhaps speaking to a stranger is not uncomfortable for another person, but it is for you. You can define what makes you feel uncomfortable, and other people can make up their own minds about what makes them feel comfortable—or uncomfortable.

Many kids think that bullying will simply go away
if they ignore it, but it won't.

Many kids think that bullying will simply go away if they ignore it, but it won't. Instead, if you are the victim of harassment or know someone who is, you need to ask an adult to intervene to put an end to it. If the bullying has just started, you can try to speak to the person who is carrying it out first to see if you can resolve it on your own. You may want to ask a trusted adult to help you prepare what to say to this person. However, if the bullying continues, you have to realize that you need help and can ask a trusted adult to get involved.

PUTTING A STOP TO BULLYING

Bullying is no longer tolerated in schools. Most states in the U.S. now have anti-bullying laws that extend to cyber bullying and activities off campus that make students feel like their school is a hostile place. In other words, bullying is not just cruel—it is also against the law, and schools are required by law to put a stop to bullying. For more information, check out this website: http://www.stopbullying.gov.

If you are being bullied or suspect that you are (or someone else is), you need to speak to a trusted adult, such as a coach, teacher, or parent. Either during a bullying episode or afterward, tell the teacher what happened. Teachers have the responsibility to report and stop bullying. If you have been the victim of physical, emotional, or sexual abuse (whether from a student, teacher, or someone else), you should report it to the teacher or to the police. Bullying can also include racism and sexism and other forms of harassment based on

WHAT DO I DO IF . . .

Question: Some kids seem to want to be my friend, but they are always making jokes and asking me to do embarrassing things like talk to a person I don't know at school. What do I do?

Answer: While it may seem like fun to be part of a group of kids, especially if they are the types of kids who like to joke around, true friends don't do things to embarrass you or laugh at you. In fact, these types of activities can be a form of bullying, even if they don't involve physical threats or violence. When you attempt to say no to participating in these types of activities, other kids may tell you that they are only joking, but you have to trust your own instincts—meaning the feeling you have deep inside. If you feel uncomfortable, this situation is not right for you. First, try telling the other kids that you don't want to put yourself in embarrassing situations; if they do not listen, you may have to find other friends who don't ask you to embarrass yourself or who laugh at you. Again, true friends don't ask you to do anything uncomfortable, and they understand when you say no.

a person's ethnic, racial, religious, sexual, or other identity, and bullying that involves these types of threats should also be reported to the police. In addition, you should know that extortion—or asking for money or other physical objects or coerced or forced actions—is illegal. If someone tries to threaten you to do something, you need to consult an adult. These activities are against the law.

UNDERSTANDING CYBERBULLYING

Cyberbullying involves harassing others through e-mail, social networking sites, text messages, and other forms of electronic technology. Like other forms of bullying, it is illegal. Cyberbullying can also include posting harassing or embarrassing photos online or sending these types of photos through e-mail or text. To prevent cyberbullying, follow these steps:

- Be sure to set up privacy settings on your e-mail and social networking sites.
- If someone is harassing you via e-mail, you can have that person blocked from sending you mail.
- Do not respond to harassing text messages, and block the sender, if possible.
- Do not post private information about yourself online. If you are posting a photo online, be sure it is appropriate and does not show you or anyone else in an embarrassing position such as not wearing clothing, drinking alcohol, or in other situations. If you are in doubt about whether a photo is appropriate to post, ask a trusted friend or adult.
- For your own protection, find out your school's policy about using and posting to intranet sites and sending e-mail. Some schools also have rules about what you can post even outside of their sites, so be sure to follow their rules.

Again, if you think you are being cyberbullied, be sure to tell a trusted adult. Just ignoring the situation will not make it stop.

SETTING GOALS

Now, it's time to set some personal goals related to recognizing and handling bullying in high school, as you might set goals when starting a video game. In order to be attainable, goals have to be SMART in nature; that is, they must be:

Specific,
Measurable,
Attainable,
Realistic, and
Timely.

Think about two or three goals you have about relating to recognizing and handling bullying in high school. You can come up with goals even if you are not facing a situation now that resembles bullying, as your goals can relate to future activities or to dealing with bullying if it does arise in the future. You can also set goals to make sure you treat other people well. Your goals can be things like, "I am not being bullied now, and I will continue to make sure that I make friends with people who make me feel good about myself," or "If a friend asks me to do something uncomfortable, I will refuse, and I will not ask other people to do things that they find uncomfortable," or "I will tell my coach or teacher if a kid sends me a threatening or embarrassing text or asks me to reveal something personal online, such as on my Facebook page." Write down one or two of your goals on a separate sheet of paper.

High school life does not always involve bullying, and, in fact, it can be a time when you connect to friends with whom you share interests and experiences. However, it's good to be aware of what bullying is and how to handle it if a situation that involves bullying arises.

5

SOCIAL MEDIA
AND ELECTRONIC
COMMUNICATION

The electronic age offers high school students new and cool ways to connect with friends and adults. You may also be a complete whiz at using online and electronic communication. Your expertise in this area is wonderful, and you should continue to use it and enjoy it. However, electronic and social media present situations in which your words create permanent and often public records, so they require you to think before acting—and before texting, e-mailing, tweeting, and posting. Read on to find ways to keep your communication via electronic media safe and socially acceptable.

QUIZ YOURSELF!
HOW WELL DO YOU UNDERSTAND ONLINE SAFETY
AND ETIQUETTE?

Answer the questions below to figure out if you handle electronic communication and social media in ways that are safe and acceptable to kids and adults:

1. When I post online or on social media sites such as Facebook or Twitter, I:
   a. Just write or post whatever comes to mind.
   b. Try to keep it clean but sometimes send photos of other people without their permission.
   c. Keep my posts clean, and ask other people before posting photos of them.
2. When someone asks me a question online, I:
   a. Answer the question, even if it involves revealing private information.
   b. Answer people I know, and send them personal information.
   c. Never send personal information, such as my address or social security number, online.
3. When someone asks to friend me online, I:
   a. Friend whomever—it's fun.
   b. Try to friend people who are at least friends of friends.
   c. Only friend people I know directly.
4. When I am sending e-mails to adults, I:
   a. Type as though I'm writing to a friend.
   b. Use abbreviations but try to be polite.
   c. Type in a formal and polite way, not using abbreviations.
5. If I have a private question, I:
   a. Post it on Facebook or another social media site.
   b. E-mail it to a bunch of people, some of whom I don't know very well.
   c. Ask a friend in person.

How to score yourself:

If you answered mostly "a": You may think that social media and online communication are the same as relating to people in real life and in person. However, social media has a public component, so you may be exposing personal information about yourself or others to people without meaning to. Read on in this chapter to develop safer ways to think about social media and online communication and more private ways to communicate with people via electronic communication.

If you answered mostly "b": You are trying to keep your online and electronic communication safe, but there may be additional ways you can safeguard what you write and post electronically. Read on for strategies to make your electronic communication even more protected and safer.

If you answered mostly "c": You are doing a good job using electronic media to communicate politely and safely with kids and adults. This chapter may offer some other suggestions to keep yourself safe online and some other ways to write to adults using electronic communication.

USING ELECTRONIC MEDIA SAFELY

There are certain rules that apply to using social networking sites and other forms of electronic communication, including e-mail and text messages. The rules are as follows:

- Do not post personal information online or send it through e-mail. Only send this type of information, which includes your address, age, social security number, credit card number, information about your bank account, and other information, to people you already know and trust. You should never share your social security number with people, unless you ask your parents first. You can also ask your parents if you are purchasing something online about how to use credit cards or other forms of payment.
- Do not post anything online that should be kept private, including personal information about you, your family, and

friends. Do not post personal photos online, and ask permission from others if you want to post photos or videos of them. Do not reveal private areas of your body in photos, or ask anyone else to do so. These areas should be kept private and do not belong online.

- When you are in doubt about posting something online, ask a parent or trusted adult. For example, a lot of people, including adults, post events online, such as going on vacations. However, this is not a good idea, as it tells people you will be away from home and therefore your house is empty. When in doubt, post less rather than more information.
- Do not take photos or videos of other people without their permission.
- Do not post insulting things about other people online, and do not send insulting e-mails or texts.
- Before sending an insulting or negative e-mail, text, or online post, be sure to think about it. Ask yourself if you should really send this information, which you cannot retract or take back. If you are in doubt, do not send it. Before sending it, ask a trusted adult if it's all right.
- Do not reveal your personal e-mail address or cell phone number to people you do not know. In addition, set privacy settings on your social networking sites so that only people you know can see your page and information.

Set privacy settings on your social networking sites so that only people you know can see your page and information.

Photos and information that you post online can be spread and copied quickly, and you never know where they are going to wind up. For example, if you send a private e-mail to one person, that person can then forward it to other people. Before putting information in an e-mail or online, think about whether you'd want it to be spread around. If not, it's better to communicate with someone by phone.

A NOTE ABOUT SOCIAL MEDIA, EMPLOYERS, AND COLLEGES

Now that you are in high school, you should realize that soon, you may be applying for a part-time or full-time job and that you may attend college. Many colleges and employers look at candidates' profiles on social networking sites such as Facebook, particularly if they have questions about that person. Do not post anything, including photos, on your Facebook page that you would not want a potential employer or college admissions office to see.

Do not post anything, including photos, on your Facebook page that you would not want a potential employer or college admissions office to see.

PRACTICING ONLINE AND CELL PHONE ETIQUETTE

In addition to keeping yourself safe online, you should keep in mind how your words affect others. You should follow **etiquette,** or rules about how to behave in social situations, online. While you may not get in trouble if you don't follow rules of etiquette, these types

WHAT DO I DO IF ...

Question: I have several photos on my Facebook page, and I'm not sure if they would look acceptable to adults or members of the public. What do I do?

Answer: If you are in doubt about whether a photo is acceptable, it's best to delete it from a potentially public place such as Facebook. You can always send it to friends privately via e-mail or text. Consult with a trusted friend or adult about which photos you should remove from your online profile.

of rules help you get along better with other people and show them that you want to be their friend.

While it's acceptable etiquette to be casual or write the way you speak on social networking sites and in texts and e-mails, you should *never* do the following:

- Don't write rude or insulting things.
- Don't make fun of people.
- Don't refer to other people's weight, bad appearance, skin color, ethnic or religious background, appearance of areas that should be private, etc. These types of comments can be understood or misunderstood as insulting or reflecting prejudice or hate on the part of the person who writes them, even if they are not intended that way.
- Don't make insulting jokes, even if you think they are funny. Remember that comments on social networking sites are permanent (though you can sometimes delete them), so think before you write.
- If you write a teacher an e-mail, be sure to follow more formal rules about writing. Don't write to a teacher the same way you

would write to a friend. See Chapter 2 for an example of how you should write to a teacher.

- If you record a greeting on your cell phone, make it polite, as you never know who will be calling you. Your greeting should include at least your first name (and possibly your last name too), so people know if they have reached the correct number.

Think before you post things online. Make sure your comments could not be interpreted as rude or insulting.

Also, consider where you use your cell phone or other mobile device. Many schools don't allow cell phones during the school day, and so you are not likely to have your phone with you. However, if you do, do not consult your phone, answer your phone, send texts, or play games while someone is speaking to you. While it is certainly tempting to answer your phone or text someone back immediately, doing so interrupts the other person and is usually considered rude (especially by adults). You can call or text the person back after your conversation is over.

When you are writing a text message, it is more appropriate to use abbreviations and not to use a title or address someone by name, as text messages are intended to be short. You generally don't send texts to teachers or to adults you don't know very well; most of the recipients of text messages are friends. Still, you should keep the following rules in mind:

- Never send an insulting text message.
- Do not use profanity or bad language in text messages (or e-mails).

85

- If the person does not know your number, be sure to say who you are in a text message.
- Using abbreviations in text messages to friends is acceptable, as long as your friends know them.
- Never text or e-mail an inappropriate photo, meaning one that reveals too much information about yourself or another person or that makes something public, including a part of your body, that should be kept private.

When you are using your phone or e-mail, it is always better to be safe than sorry. Try to keep your communication polite, and consider the person you are speaking to or writing to when deciding how to express yourself.

SETTING GOALS

Now, it's time to set some personal goals related to sending electronic communication and using social media in ways that are safe and polite. In order to be attainable, goals have to be SMART in nature; that is, they must be:

Specific,
Measurable,
Attainable,
Realistic, and
Timely.

Think about two or three goals you have about using electronic and social media. Your goals can be things like, "Within the next week, I will delete any photos from my Facebook account that I wouldn't want everyone to see," or "I will write to my teachers using complete introductions and without abbreviations." Write down two or three goals on a separate piece of paper.

While you may find electronic media a very friendly and convenient way of connecting with other kids and adults, you always want to be aware that a lot of people you don't know can look at what you write and that there are different rules for communicating with adults than there are for communicating with kids.

6

DEVELOPING
HEALTHY HABITS

In this chapter, we will look at how healthy your habits are. These kinds of habits help you feel better both mentally and physically, and they help you reach your potential in school and in activities outside of school. You may have already heard parents or teachers reminding you (or even nagging you!) to get enough sleep, exercise, eat well, and find time to relax, and you may have grown tired of these types of reminders. What you may not realize is that if you adopt some of these healthier habits, you may feel better about yourself, look better, feel less stressed and more relaxed, and even perform better—in school, sports, and other activities. In addition, in this chapter, you will get some ideas about how to dress and style yourself and to look good in your eyes and those of your peers.

First, start by thinking about your health habits and take this quiz about yourself.

QUIZ YOURSELF!
HOW WELL DO YOU FOLLOW HEALTHY HABITS?

Answer the questions below to assess your health habits.

1. For the most part, I tend to eat:
   a. The same types of foods every day, especially bland foods like bread and noodles.
   b. A little bit of healthy food, such as fruit and vegetables, and a lot of junk food like candy.
   c. Foods from different groups, such as fruits, vegetables, lean meat, dairy, and a few sweets.
2. On a regular basis, I:
   a. Am very keyed up or unable to relax.
   b. Feel wound up after school but try to relax by listening to music, watching movies, or playing video games.
   c. Use some tried-and-true ways to calm down, including reading, yoga, exercise, and writing in a journal.
3. When it comes to getting enough sleep, I:
   a. Tend to go to bed late after staying up reading, playing video games, or doing some other activity.
   b. Try to get to bed early but toss and turn and don't get enough sleep.
   c. Turn off electronic devices and get to bed early and usually get about 8 or 9 hours of sleep a night.
4. To get ready for school in the morning, I:
   a. Run out the door without looking at myself in the mirror.
   b. Take a few minutes to brush my teeth and comb my hair.
   c. Leave enough time to think about what I'm going to wear, get clean clothes, and style my hair the way I want it to look.

5. With regard to smoking, I:
   a. Have started to smoke cigarettes.
   b. Sometimes smoke at parties or when around other people who smoke.
   c. Have decided that smoking is not a healthy habit and do not want to try it.

How to score yourself:

If you answered mostly "a": You may be treating your body and yourself relatively badly. It doesn't mean that it's too late to learn some healthier ways to eat, get enough sleep, and relax. Start by changing one part of your life, whether it's your diet or how much sleep you get, and see if it makes you feel better. If so, you can consider making changes in other areas of your life.

If you answered mostly "b": You may have guessed that you are already taking some important steps to feeling good, physically and emotionally. Read this chapter to get ideas for other steps you might implement over time to maximize your energy and your health.

If you answered mostly "c": You already have many healthy habits and are working actively to find ways to relax and relieve stress (though that may seem like a contradiction in terms). You may find some other ideas in this chapter to build on your healthy habits.

GETTING ENOUGH SLEEP

Research has shown that many children and adults with Asperger's struggle with sleep problems and disorders. In fact, studies have documented that about 75% of kids with Asperger's have trouble sleeping.[1] While scientists are still trying to figure out why this true, there is no doubt that if you struggle with sleeping, you are not alone. (You may find that you sleep just fine, however!) Not getting enough sleep not only makes you feel tired, it can also make you feel down and interfere with your concentration during the school day. It is estimated that most teenagers need eight and a half to nine hours of sleep per night, though people vary a bit in how much they need. You may think you are doing fine on less sleep, but try getting a full night's sleep and see how you feel. You will likely find that you feel much better.

It is estimated that most teenagers need eight and a half to nine hours of sleep per night, though people vary a bit in how much they need.

Many people try to make up for lack of sleep by drinking caffeine during the day or at night or by taking naps when they get home from school before they do their homework. However, these practices tend to interfere with sleep at night. Generally, you should avoid caffeine, particularly in the afternoon or at night. Be aware that the sweetened coffee drinks available at many coffee stores have a lot of caffeine, which can keep you awake for many hours after you drink them.

In addition, if you really have to take a nap in the afternoon, try to limit it to about 20 minutes or less. Even a short nap can help you feel refreshed but will not interfere with your sleep at night,

---

[1]Goldberg, M. A., & Berkman, J. (n.d.). *Sleep problems in children with Asperger syndrome.* Retrieved from Asperger's Association of New England website: http://www.aane.org/asperger_resources/articles/children_parenting/sleep_problems_asperger.html

the way a one- or two-hour nap will. Many teenagers get into a sleep cycle in which they stay up late, take long naps when they get home, and spend days feeling like zombies. To make up for lost sleep time, they sleep late on the weekends, but this pattern only makes them groggy on the weekends and sleep-deprived during the week. In order to break this cycle, you have to forgo an afternoon nap, or just take a short 20-minute nap if necessary, and get to bed at the same time each night. Eventually, your sleep cycle should re-set itself, allowing you to fall asleep earlier and get up without feeling groggy in the morning.

Here are some tips that may be able to help you get the sleep you need:

- Turn off electronics. Though it may seem tempting to play video games or watch movies when you can't sleep, looking at the light on the screen may stimulate the brain to think it's day-time and therefore to stay awake. Experts recommend turning off screens an hour before bedtime. By the way, you should also be careful not to charge cell phones, iPads, and other devices where you can see their glow, as sleep experts believe that even ambient, or surrounding, light can keep you awake at night.
- Decrease exercise before bedtime. While exercise is a great way to reduce stress, you should try to exercise earlier in the day, as exercising later at night can keep you awake.
- If you have difficulty falling asleep, use relaxation techniques such as taking a hot bath, meditating, reading, listening to music, or writing in a journal before bed. Again, while many teenagers watch movies or play video games or post on Facebook when they can't sleep, these techniques only keep you awake at night. If you are tempted to respond to friends' text messages at night, put your phone in another room so it won't disturb you at night.

- Avoid caffeine, especially in the later afternoon or night, as it can last in your system for hours and keep you awake. Keep in mind that alcohol and tobacco can also interfere with sleep.

Let's consider the case of Danny, a sophomore in high school who spent most days feeling like a zombie. He routinely went to bed around midnight and had to get up at 6:30 am to get to school on time. When he got home around 4 or 4:30 pm, he fell asleep for an hour, and then he texted his friends, looked at Facebook, and played video games until dinner time at 7. After dinner, he liked to watch his favorite TV shows and finally sat down to work around 9 or 9:30. When he was done at 11, he would play video games until he felt tired.

It's clear that Danny is more interested in playing video games, watching TV, and keeping up with his friends than he is in getting a good night's sleep. This is understandable. It can be hard to spend all day in school and then spend time at night doing homework. It sometimes means you have to sacrifice time playing video games and watching movies. However, the problem is that if you don't sleep, you feel pretty terrible the next day. Let's look at how Danny changed his sleep habits to feel better and still find some time for video games and other fun activities:

Danny decided not to take a nap when he got home from school at 4:30 (or 5:30 on days when he had basketball practice or games). Instead, he took a break for 15 minutes and shot some hoops outside to feel more energized. Then, he did homework for an hour or an hour and a half before dinner at 7. In addition, he tried to get some of his work done at school during study hall so he had less to do at home. After dinner, he usually had two hours to play video games, watch TV, and listen to music. He decided to turn off all his electronic devices at 10 and put his phone in another room so he wouldn't feel tempted to answer texts or respond to Facebook posts. Instead, he listened to music or read until lights out at 10:30.

He woke up at 6:30 the next morning feeling more energized and not as groggy. As a result, he found he could concentrate better in school, and his basketball game improved, too. He also found that he felt less stressed in general.

With a bit of planning, Danny still had time to play video games, relax, get his homework done, and get a good night's sleep. A good night's sleep is one way to help reduce stress. Read on to find other ways to feel more relaxed, even when school gets very busy and stressful.

WHAT DO I DO IF ...

Question: I play video games almost all the time when I'm not in school. It's gotten to the point where video games interfere with my sleep. What do I do?
Answer: Video games are fun, but if you play them all the time, you will be cutting out other important parts of your life, including not only your homework and schoolwork, but also friends, family, sleep, exercise, reading, and other activities. Signs that you have a problem with video games or the internet—or even a video game addiction—are that you are only happy when playing video games or on the Internet, you can't sleep, or you are continually thinking about the video game you are playing instead of about your friends, schoolwork, or reading. In addition to hurting your social life (while it's true that you can play with other people online, these experiences aren't the same as hanging out with other kids in person), playing video games all the time is unhealthy. Staring at a computer screen for too long can interfere with your sleep, and not getting enough sleep can harm your health. Try to limit your video game playing to about an hour each day, and see if you start to feel better. If you find you can't limit your video game playing, you may need to speak to a parent or another adult, and you may have to disconnect your games for a period of time until you can limit your playing time. Spend time outside, away from screens, and see if you enjoy your time away from the screen. If you would like help, visit the website of On-line Gamers Anonymous at http://www.olganon.org/, which is a self-help organization to help people whose lives have been taken over by gaming.

REDUCING STRESS

We tend to think of stress as a negative thing. After all, who wouldn't prefer a summer Saturday when you feel little stress and all you have to do is figure out which video game to play, which song to listen to, or which book to read? However, a manageable bit of stress can help you get work done. If you didn't have a test, for example, you probably wouldn't be that motivated to study. But when stress gets excessive, it can make you feel tired, depressed, and paralyzed or unable to get anything done.

In addition, some children and adults with Asperger's have added layers of stress because they find parts of the school or work day very stressful. Some people with Asperger's react with stress to **sensory input,** which refers to input that comes through your five senses (hearing, sight, touch, taste, and smell). For example, some people with Asperger's react to loud noises, too much noise over a long period of time, strange smells, or bright lights. They may also have difficulty dealing with other people all day. They may need to take a break after a day of relating to others, and taking a few moments of solitude may help them. In addition, some people with Asperger's find changes in routine or schedules difficult to handle, so they need more time to adjust, react, and unwind after periods of change or disruption in their schedules.

If you are going through a time of stress or anticipate that a time of change is approaching, you can plan ahead for such a time, such as a concert you have to perform in or a test you have to take. Be sure to block out times for relaxation and schedule them, much the same way you could plan a doctor's appointment or study time.

Here are some ideas for ways to relax, particularly during stressful times:

- Make sure you get enough sleep, typically eight and a half to nine hours a night (see above).

- Plan time for exercise, particularly in the morning or afternoon. It has been shown that exercise, even moderate exercise such as walking briskly, can improve people's mood all day, help them feel more relaxed, and help them sleep better! You may notice that after exercising, you feel less worried and more energized. Even if you don't like group sports, you can find other activities that you enjoy, such as yoga, karate or tae kwon do, hiking, golf, swimming, surfing, skateboarding, walking, or working out in the gym while listening to music. Swimming is a particularly good way to exercise, reduce stress, and perhaps even make your senses feel better.

- Try strategies to reduce sensory input—if they are allowed— such as wearing a hat or visor in class, or wearing headphones in certain situations such as concerts. You may also need to take "sensory breaks" in a dark room, to relax after a lot of exposure to bright lights and loud noises. These are accommodations, or changes, that you may have to work out with your teacher or other people in school. For example, your teachers may allow you to take a break in a dark classroom during part of lunch. You can also use these strategies to relax after school.

- Practice deep breathing. Deep breathing is a process by which you inhale through your nose, let your belly fill with air for a few seconds, and breathe out slowly through your mouth. It can help you feel more relaxed in a few seconds. You can practice this relaxation technique without those around you noticing, so it's a good way to try to relax in school or other public places. You may need to repeat this process several times over a course of two to three minutes to feel more relaxed.

- Try journaling or drawing to work out some of your stress. Writing down your thoughts, or sketching about your thoughts, ideas, and worries, can be a good way to get all your interesting thoughts down on paper and to relax your mind.

- Don't procrastinate. Procrastination, or putting off your work, can actually cause more stress than just getting to work. Even if you can just do one part of a project or a large assignment like a paper, the act of getting started will help you get moving and maybe reduce your stress and worry.
- Talk to someone. If you are excessively worried to the point that your stress starts to interfere with your daily functioning, such as your ability to have fun, sleep, or eat, be sure to talk to a parent or trusted adult.

Stress is a normal part of everyday life, and part of making yourself feel more comfortable in high school involves finding ways to deal with stress. However, if you feel that nothing is helping to lessen your stress, you need to speak with your parents or another trusted adult about getting help.

Now, let's look at how Henry reduced his stress level in high school. Henry was a worried kid during his freshman year of high school. He was in a new school, and he didn't know too many kids

WHAT DO I DO IF …

Question: I have trouble handling the bright lights and loud noises at school. What do I do?

Answer: Fluorescent lights can be a problem for people with struggle with sensory problems, or taking in more input through their senses than they can comfortably handle. In order to deal with these problems, ask your teachers' permission to wear a cap or visor at school. Explain to them that you are not trying to be disrespectful but that you need the cap to feel comfortable in school. You can also wear ear plugs or headphones during certain times at school, with your teachers' permission, or take breaks to walk in a quiet part of the school, if possible. For example, you can take breaks in the library or another place such as a guidance counselor's office.

at first and was trying to make friends. He also was trying to finish all his work, but he found his freshman English class very confusing. To top it all off, he was getting home later than he was used to because of participating on the wrestling team, and he often got to bed really late and didn't have time to listen to music, watch movies, or play video games—all the things he found relaxing.

Henry's life seemed really stressful, and if he didn't even have enough time to relax, how would he begin reducing the stress in his life? It seemed difficult, but here are some of the steps he took:

After feeling depressed over the weekend, Henry finally decided to talk to his parents about how stressed out he felt. He told them honestly that he didn't know what to do and that he wasn't trying to avoid his work, just trying to figure out how to do it better. In talking over the situation with them, he realized that he had felt better at his middle school. When his parents asked him to think about why that was, he realized that he had known more kids in middle school and that the classrooms weren't as loud.

Henry's parents helped him develop some strategies for what he could do differently. First, Henry decided to ask his teachers if he could wear headphones during study hall. He did not listen to music, but his headphones cancelled out some of the noise around him, and he was able to relax for a 45-minute period each day and get some of his homework done. That way, he had less work to do at home, and he was able to work on a nightly schedule for his homework so that he could finish his work more efficiently and find time for relaxing, reading, and playing video games. Henry tried to get to bed a bit earlier because he found that he felt better when he was rested. He also decided to go out with some of the kids on his wrestling team over the weekend, and he began to feel as though he had more friends and people to talk to at school. Finally, though he was scared at first, he decided to approach his English teacher for help on his papers. Henry's English teacher suggested a method of outlining his papers that made his writing better and faster, not only resulting in higher grades but also in more time to relax, hang out with his friends, and play video games. Looking back, Henry realized that he was happy he had spoken to his parents about his stress. Getting totally stressed out had actually helped motivate him to think about ways to handle his stress better!

Here are some strategies that Henry used to deal with his stress. Consider whether any of them might help you:

- He decided to speak to his parents when he felt stressed out so they could help him think about other ways to handle his work and stress level.
- He wore noise-canceling headphones during study hall to help him get more work done during the school day, so he had more time to relax at home.
- He used his free time to relax and play video games and do other activities he enjoyed.
- He asked his English teacher for help so he could earn better grades and finish his work more efficiently.
- He approached kids on his sports team to develop more friendships.

Can you think of any other strategies that you can use to reduce your stress? If so, write them down on another piece of paper, on your phone, or on a post-it that you can refer to when you are feeling stressed out.

EATING A BALANCED DIET

Believe it or not, the food you eat can also make you feel more relaxed—or more stressed out. That doesn't mean you need to eat things you don't like. After all, it is perfectly natural for everyone to have specific likes and dislikes with regard to food. Some people crave steak, while others are vegetarian and do not eat meat. Some people prefer spicy foods, while others like a bland diet. You most likely have certain comfort foods, or foods you enjoy and turn to when you are feeling down, and that is all right in principle. However, many people with Asperger's struggle with the smell and texture of certain foods. This can make it hard to eat a balanced diet, meaning a healthy diet with a variety of foods, including vegetables and fruit, whole grains (such as whole-wheat bread or brown rice), dairy, and lean meats and fish. You may find that you struggle to eat foods that have a strong smell or a certain texture (whether it's crunchy or mushy foods).

A bit of experimentation may help you develop a fuller, more balanced diet. Here are some examples:

- If you struggle to eat fruit and vegetables, try a smoothie so that the foods will be blended together and smooth.
- If you like breads or pasta, try whole-grain or whole-wheat pastas, which are more nutritious than the white-flour variety.
- Start slowly with eating new foods, and take small bites. Don't chomp right into a new food without knowing how it's going to taste and feel to you—and to your mouth.
- If you can't stomach vegetables, trying mixing them in small amounts into foods you like, such as pizza or pasta sauce. Even a small amount of veggies is better than none.
- If you like the texture of a certain food, such as gummy bears, try a healthier version of that food, such as natural fruit snacks.
- If you don't like milk, try chocolate milk or soy milk.
- Try to eat healthy foods in your school cafeteria, or bring your lunch from home if there are no healthy options you like at school.
- If you are struggling to eat a healthy diet, consult with the nurse at your school or with your doctor for some tips. You

may need to consult with a doctor if you have food allergies so that you can develop a healthy diet that does not involve food you are allergic to.

Can you think of three new healthy foods that you want to try? If so, jot them down on a separate piece of paper. Challenge yourself to try one of these new foods each week.

Eating healthy foods is important not only for your long-term health but also for the way you feel each day. If you eat a healthy, balanced diet, you will likely feel more energized. It is particularly important to start each day with a balanced breakfast, such as whole-wheat toast and peanut butter (if you are not allergic to nuts) or egg whites and a fruit, to give you energy to take on the day. Again, if you can't stomach these foods in the morning, try a smoothie with yogurt and fruit. If none of those foods appeal to you, consult with your doctor or school nurse to try to find healthier alternatives.

You also want to think about what you eat in the afternoon if you are feeling tired or need a lift. Many kids turn to sweetened coffee drinks for mid-afternoon snacks because they look and taste good and give people a temporary rush from all the caffeine and sugar. However, these types of drinks, in addition to sugary foods and snacks, generally result in a crash about an hour after consuming them, and the caffeine in coffee drinks can keep you awake at night, even hours after you've consumed it. Try to experiment with other types of mid-afternoon snacks, such as smoothies, whole-wheat bread with peanut butter or hummus, or yogurt.

A NOTE ABOUT ALCOHOL AND DRUGS

In high school, you may find many of your classmates are trying out alcohol and even drugs at parties. You may also find that some kids smoke cigarettes. There are a lot of different reasons people start trying these substances. Many people think they feel more relaxed and more able to socialize with others if they have had a drink or a cigarette. Others think that drinking and smoking will make them look cooler. If you feel anxious about fitting in or just feel anxious and worried in general, alcohol and cigarettes will not fix these problems but will make them worse in the long run, as alcohol and substances in cigarettes (such as nicotine) can actually worsen your anxiety. In fact, there are many negative consequences of under-age drinking, including social, academic, and even legal problems.[2]

If you feel anxious about fitting in or just feel anxious and worried in general, alcohol will not fix these problems but will make them worse in the long run, as alcohol and substances in cigarettes (such as nicotine) can actually worsen your anxiety.

You should do research about these substances and speak to your parents or a trusted adult about them. You may already know that alcohol and drugs such as marijuana can be harmful to developing brains and that you should never use these substances when driving. Smoking cigarettes is harmful to your short-term and long-term health. Cigarettes can decrease your performance in sports and cause breathing problems, and other health concerns. If you have concerns about your use or other kids' use of these substances, speak to a parent or another adult whose advice you value.

---

[2]Centers for Disease Control and Prevention (2014, January 16). *Fact Sheets: Underage Drinking.* Retrieved from http://www.cdc.gov/alcohol/fact-sheets/underage-drinking.htm

If you are at a party and someone offers you a drink or cigarette that you want to decline, try the following lines:

- "No, thank you." (Sometimes, a simple "no" might work.)
- "No, I'm driving tonight." (In the case of someone offering you a drink.)
- "No, I'm in training for sports."
- "No, thanks. I have asthma, so I can't smoke." (Or you can mention another health problem that prevents you from smoking or drinking.)
- "I just don't feel like it now." (If the other person persists.)

Try to say these lines calmly but firmly, as people might persist if they sense you are flustered or unsure. If these lines don't work, it may be a sign that you are hanging out with people who aren't really your friends because they don't value your needs.

DRESSING AND STYLING YOURSELF

Now that you're in high school, it's time to develop your own individual style and look. You may not have given much thought to the way you look yet, or you may have spent hours in front of the mirror trying to figure out what looks best on you. If your parents are still choosing your clothes, or if you haven't yet found your own style, it's time to start thinking about how you want to look and dress.

If you aren't sure how you want to cut and style your hair, take a look at the kids around you, and consult some magazines. You can also speak to the person who cuts your hair to get some ideas for haircuts that are flattering for your face shape. Your hair dresser can also suggest hair products if you are interested in styling your hair a certain way. While it may be tempting to wear your hair in your face, which provides some protection from people you are speaking to, people want to see your face when you are speaking with them.

If you are interested in wearing makeup, you can get a makeup consultation in a cosmetics store or at the makeup counter in a department store.

If you wear glasses, look for a style that flatters the shape of your face and that does not hide your features. You may want to ask a stylish friend to help you pick out a pair of glasses that looks good on you.

You may be concerned with how the material of your clothes feels. It's totally fine to look for clothes that feel comfortable. If you wear jeans every day, look for the types of cuts that are in style, and, if department stores are too expensive, look for similar styles in second-hand or consignment stores. If you aren't sure what's in style or what looks good on you, ask a friend who has good style to go shopping with you. Shoes or sneakers can also be a critical part of your look, so, again, if you are unsure about what to buy, you can consider going shopping with a friend who has good taste.

Make sure you have a few outfits for formal occasions, such as a long-sleeved button-down shirt and tie for guys and a formal dress, or pants and a nice top, for girls. You should also have a pair of dress shoes that matches your formal outfit. Ask a trusted friend to come shopping for outfits with you, and shop in second-hand or consignment stores if price is an issue.

Even when dressing formally, you can find comfortable clothing. If you are going to wear a shirt or dress all day, make sure it not only fits you, but that it also feels right. You can buy formal clothes in comfortable, non-scratchy fabrics like cotton. Avoid synthetics and some wool blends, which tend not to be as comfortable and don't breathe as easily. After you've purchased an item, remove the tags on the backs of shirts or dresses if the tags bother you. Though it may seem annoying to try clothes on in the store, you should do so and walk around in them to see how comfortable they are. Consider that you are going to have to wear these clothes for a long time, so think realistically about how they feel.

If shopping for clothes in a store is too overwhelming, try ordering online, particularly if the place you are buying from has a free shipping and return policy. Ordering online is a way to avoid long lines, noise, and fluorescent lights in department stores; however, be sure to try your clothes on for size and comfort before you have to wear them. If they don't fit or feel right, return them within the allowable time frame.

Before you go to school each morning, make sure you do the following:

- Take a shower (or take it the night before).
- Brush your teeth.
- Brush your hair and style it the way you want it to look. You may need mousse or gel to get the look you want, so speak with your hair stylist about which products to use.
- Apply deodorant.
- Make sure your clothes are clean and unwrinkled. If you do not want to iron your clothes, purchase wrinkle-free clothes.
- If it is difficult or time-consuming to choose your clothes, pick out your outfits the night before and leave them neatly on your dresser.
- If you are a guy, you may want to start shaving during high school, so ask your parents or a friend who shaves about the best products to use.

If you forget any of these steps, put them on a post-it or dry-erase board where you can see them in the morning.

SETTING GOALS

Now, it's time to set some personal goals about healthy habits, as you might set goals when starting a video game. In order to be attainable, goals have to be SMART in nature; that is, they must be:

Specific,
Measurable,
Attainable,
Realistic, and
Timely.

You may decide on goals such as, "I will try to eat more fruits and vegetables in creative ways such as smoothies or sauces," or "I will try some deep breathing exercises when I'm feeling stressed at school," or "I will speak to my teacher about wearing head phones during study hall to feel calmer and get more work done." Your goals are up to you. Try to write down three SMART goals on a separate sheet of paper.

High school can be a time when you not only learn information that prepares you for later life, but when you also learn habits that can keep you healthy and happy as an adult. It can also be a time to start defining your personal style, just as you are starting to define yourself and your personality. That doesn't mean you can't change later, but if you adopt healthy habits and flattering styles now, you may decide to keep some of these styles and habits into adulthood.

7

HANDLING EMOTIONS

Everyone is overcome with strong emotions at times, whether pleasant emotions such as happiness or contentment, or uncomfortable emotions such as anger, frustration, sadness, or anxiety. While you may not be able to stop these emotions, it is possible to learn strategies to handle them, which is particularly important during the school day and in public places. This chapter may give you some ideas about how to understand the triggers that may set off strong emotions in you and some techniques for handling these emotions.

QUIZ YOURSELF!
HOW WELL DO YOU HANDLE EMOTIONS?

Answer the questions below to figure out how well you handle strong emotions and upset feelings.

1. When I get upset, it is because of:
   a. Things I don't really understand; I just get upset without understanding why.

b. Other people making me angry.

c. Triggers such as feeling tired, hungry, or lonely—and I understand why I feel upset.

2. When I do poorly on a test or assignment, I:

a. Usually hit a wall or punch myself.

b. Get really mad at the teacher and myself.

c. Get upset but then try to speak to the teacher and go over the test a few days later.

3. When I do badly on a test, I also think to myself:

a. "I will never, ever get into college or have a good job."

b. "I may not be able to recover."

c. "I can improve my grade by preparing for the next test."

4. When the lunchroom or a class is too loud, I:

a. Put my hands over my ears.

b. Take a walk in the hallway.

c. Have designated spots, such as an empty classroom or the library, where I know I can find a quiet space and where teachers allow me to go.

5. When I feel angry at a friend, I:

a. Yell at that person.

b. Walk away from that person.

c. Walk away but return to speak when I feel calmer.

How to score yourself:

If you answered mostly "a": As you might realize, strong emotions tend to overtake you at school, and when you are interacting with friends and teachers. Read on in this chapter to identify some common triggers that might cause these strong emotions and to explore some strategies for dealing with your strong emotions.

If you answered mostly "b": You have developed some good strategies for dealing with strong emotions. A lot of your strategies involve understanding your emotions, but you may not have a good way to resolve them or to feel better. Read on to learn some ways you might handle these emotions in order to feel more positive and take a more active stance towards dealing with problems in the future.

If you answered mostly "c": You not only understand what sets you off, but you also have developed some very good strategies for dealing with strong emotions—strategies that help you feel better, resolve problems, and relate better to other people. Read on in this chapter to see if any of the other strategies might help you build on the good coping skills you already have.

YOUR BODY'S REACTION TO STRESS

You may not be aware that you are starting to feel stressed until you reach a point at which you are very angry or upset. However, there are warning signs that your body is starting to feel stressed. If you notice these warning signs, you may be able to avoid reaching a kind of "emotional boiling point," which is the point at which you feel so upset and angry that you cannot handle the situation you are in very well. Much like you can turn down the temperature on a pot of water to keep it from coming to a boil, if you recognize that you are starting to feel stressed or upset, you may find ways to cool yourself off and avoid reaching your emotional boiling point.

Along the way to reaching your boiling point, you may experience some of the following warning signs:

- You may feel your face getting hot or flushed.
- You may start to tremble.
- You may start to feel dizzy.
- Your throat might get dry.
- Your hands might turn clammy or cold.
- You may start to sweat.
- You may start to cry or tear up.
- You may have difficulty swallowing.

- Your muscles, particularly in your shoulders, may feel tight or painful. You may notice your shoulders are higher than they should be because your muscles are not relaxed.

These are all clues or signs that you may be starting to get upset, anxious, or angry. Here are some ways you can cool down:

- Take a break or a walk, if possible. The act of walking, even for 10 or 15 minutes, can help clear your mind and relax your muscles. Taking a walk during the school day may only be possible during lunch or break times, of course, but you can also take a walk before or after school to calm your mind.
- Try some deep breathing exercises in which you take in a breath through your nose while watching your stomach rise, hold it for about three counts, and then release it slowly through your mouth. Try to imagine your anger or anxiety flowing out with your breath.
- If you are in a place where you can do some stretching or yoga poses, these types of exercises can help you relax. Try letting your hands hang down in front of you as you bend at the waist. Shake out your hands to release some tension. You can also try some wall push-ups, pushing yourself off the wall a few times.
- Use a **sensory tool,** such as a squishy ball or beads, that you can carry in your pocket and play with without other people noticing. These types of tools can help you calm your senses and give you something repetitive to do that takes your mind off your anxiety or anger.
- Try to listen to some calming music on your headphones.
- If you are feeling tired or worn out, try to take a nap. Sleep can relax your mind.
- You can try **visualizing,** or imagining a scene that is peaceful— whether it is an open field, a beach, or your bedroom. It some-

times helps to close your eyes, and think about what it would feel like to be in that place—for example, the sea breezes ruffling your hair, the feeling of the sand and the water, etc.

- You can also try to **visualize** yourself in a bubble, or away from other people, if the feeling of being around others is too overwhelming or upsetting at the moment.
- Try writing or drawing about your frustrating feelings. Writing and drawing are wonderful ways to help you make sense of frustration and get some of the feelings out of your system.
- Try to relax your muscles by concentrating on each area of your body, working your way from your head to your toes. Focus on tensing and then relaxing each part of your body, one part at a time. Relax each area and let the tension leave your body.
- Exercise is a great way to clear your mind and let go of stress; after playing sports or working out, you can often look at a

WHAT DO I DO IF ...

Question: Sometimes, I get so frustrated if I'm not good at something that I want to hurt myself, yell, or have a tantrum. What do I do?

Answer: While these reactions are understandable in certain situations (though it is never acceptable to hurt yourself or others), by the time you get to high school, you should be able to control your emotions fairly well most of the time. In addition, losing control in front of other people can be really embarrassing. If you feel like you are on the verge of losing control, try to take a break. Take a brisk walk to get rid of some of your energy. If you are in class, you may need to ask permission to take a break. Send yourself reassuring messages and remind yourself that no one is perfect. Try writing or drawing about this situation after the fact to process it in your mind. Think about how it felt in the minute and how you might handle the situation differently in the future. If you revisit the situation when you are calmer, you will likely be able to think about other ways to handle that same situation in a more productive way.

situation more clearly. You don't need to play sports if you don't want to; you can go for a brisk walk, work out at the gym, swim, or go for a run.

A NOTE ON STIM BEHAVIORS

Some people with Asperger's engage in what is called **"stim"** or **"stimulation" behavior.** They often clap, jump, or do other repetitive behaviors that soothe them. These types of behaviors are fine to continue to practice in private (for example, when you are in your room), but as you move into high school, you may want to try to use other behaviors in public. Other people may not understand why you are clapping, tapping, or jumping repeatedly when no one else is, and you may feel uncomfortable doing so. Try to find some behaviors to replace these "stim behaviors." For example, instead of jumping or clapping, try using a **sensory tool** such as a soft fabric or squishy ball to soothe your senses. Try to choose a tool that you can use privately or keep in your pocket, as you may not want other people to see it. While there is nothing wrong with using a squishy ball or another similar device, you may want to avoid discussing them or having to explain them to other people.

WHAT SETS YOU OFF? UNDERSTANDING YOUR TRIGGERS

Much as a trigger sets off a trap, there are emotional **triggers** that set off negative emotions in people. A trigger is a situation or event that causes someone to feel upset or overwhelmed.

Everyone's triggers are different—for example, some people feel agitated or upset when they hear loud noises, while others love loud noises. In general, however, triggers are things that make you feel alone, misunderstood, mistreated, or unable to handle what you are dealing with.

Common responses that will not help the situation include:

- Hitting things
- Hitting yourself or other people
- Losing control in public
- Saying things you don't mean
- Doing things you might regret or that are dangerous.

More helpful responses include:

- Taking a deep breath.
- Removing yourself from difficult situations.
- Walking away from the situation and coming back to it later, or speaking to the people involved in the situation later.
- Taking a walk, which helps you calm down and think about the situation more clearly.
- Speaking to a trusted friend or adult about the situation.
- Writing about the situation in your journal.

Here are some common triggers that might set you off in school. Think about how you would react to each situation and how you handle it. Consider whether there are other strategies, or ways of responding, to each situation that might help you feel better, resolve the situation, and perhaps even avoid the situation in the future.

Trigger: You perform poorly on an assignment or test.

Common Responses: Common responses to receiving a poor grade are to hide or crumple up your assignment, hit the wall (or something else), start to cry or tear up, blame the teacher for your grade, or engage in overly negative thinking. You may be tempted to use **all-or-nothing thinking,** which means that you see everything in one extreme or another without realizing that there are other possible ways to look at a situation that lie more in the middle. For example, you may think that if you fail one test, you will never get into college or get a good job, which is not true. You may also feel like your parents or teachers will be very disappointed in you.

Helpful Strategies: Here are some more effective ways to deal with this situation, ways that help you resolve the problem and perhaps even avoid it in the future:

- Meet with the teacher, go over your test, and speak about how to prepare differently next time.
- Work hard on the next assignment.
- Figure out what you did wrong and change how you prepare. Remember, you are responsible for your grade—not your teacher. You may easily be able to fix the issue by realizing that you did not understand your teacher's directions, for example. Students often make this type of mistake in high school, and you are not expected to be perfect. The mistakes you make in high school will help you understand how to prepare for future courses and to become a better student.
- Realize that one failed test is not going to affect the rest of your life and that your parents and teachers will not judge you based on one grade.
- Take some time to relax and revisit the test in the morning when you feel calmer and better rested.

Trigger: You have a very frustrating conversation with a friend, and you feel like you have no friends who understand you.

Common Responses: It is frustrating when friends don't seem to understand you. If you get into an angry discussion or a fight with a friend, you may think that this friend will never understand you or that none of your friends understand you. Again, this is an example of **all-or-nothing thinking,** which means seeing things in very dire, black-and-white terms.

Helpful Strategies: Here are some other ways to consider handling this situation:

- It's very difficult to think clearly when you are angry or upset. Try sleeping on the situation, and think about it in the morning, when you may feel calmer.
- Ask yourself if you are engaging in all-or-nothing thinking. For example, just because you had a fight with one friend, does it really mean that no one understands you or even that this friend never understands you? You may start to realize that the situation is not as bad as you first thought.
- Try to approach your friend when you feel calmer and have a little more distance from the situation. If possible, you can speak to a trusted friend or adult to get their opinion.

Trigger: You are trying to do something that isn't easy, whether it is writing a paper or learning how to shoot a basket, and it gets so frustrating that you want to scream.

Common Responses: You may feel incredibly frustrated when you can't do something, whether the task is mental or physical. You may feel tempted to scream, hit yourself or an object, or even have a tantrum. While that is understandable, you have to try to cool yourself down and handle this situation calmly. This is especially important in school, because schools do not allow this type of behavior, and it may be embarrassing to act this way in front of other people.

Helpful Strategies: Instead, try some of these strategies:

- If you feel yourself getting upset, step away from the activity and take a break.
- Return to the activity when you are feeling calmer, and perhaps ask the help of a teacher, friend or parent.

- Send calming messages to yourself. Remind yourself that no one does everything perfectly all the time. You may do better with some help and practice.
- As always when upset, concentrate on your breathing. Focus on breathing deeply and filling your lungs and letting out your breath slowly. You may have to repeat these breathing exercises several times until you feel calmer.
- Try to draw or write about your frustration rather than taking it out on yourself, an object, or another person.

Trigger: You have an event at school or elsewhere that is really loud, making you feel overwhelmed.

Common Responses: You may feel tempted to leave such an event, or, if you stay, you may feel upset and agitated. This is an example of a situation in which there is too much **sensory input,** or information coming in through your five senses. Sometimes, too much light, noise, movement, or even strong smells may make you feel upset. Many people with Asperger's feel overwhelmed in such situations—as do many people without Asperger's—and it's totally natural to want to run away.

Helpful Strategies: Here are some other ways you might consider handling the event:

- Try to find out in advance from your teachers if there is going to be a loud event. If so, ask permission to take a break from the event if needed or to wear ear plugs or headphones.
- If you can, try to sit in the back at such events, or away from the source of noise.
- With permission from your teacher, wear a visor or hat to block out bright lights.
- In the cafeteria, sit far away from where food is being prepared to minimize your exposure to strong smells.

Trigger: Your schedule at school changes without much warning, and you are dealing with unexpected changes in your routine.

Common Responses: It can be difficult to handle changes in your routine, particularly if they are unexpected. You may respond, understandably, by feeling upset, confused, and agitated.

Helpful Strategies: Here are some possible ways to handle this type of situation:

- Again, ask your teachers in advance if there any days or times when your regular schedule will be changed.
- If you are facing a change in routine, ask your teachers for a preview of what will happen so you will know what to expect.
- Ask your teachers in advance for permission to take a break when needed, on days when your routine changes.
- Use deep breathing techniques, including taking a deep breath, holding it for about three counts, and letting it out. Deep breathing can help you relax in the moment, and you can use this technique to calm yourself down without other people even noticing.
- If you are wondering how to react to changes, try to observe some of your classmates who seem to handle these types of situations well.
- If you feel as though you didn't handle this situation as well as you might have, be sure to speak to a trusted friend or adult about how you could handle the situation better next time. Don't be too hard on yourself; just think about how you might change your reaction in the future.

Now, think about some of your common triggers. Write down three of them on a sheet of paper.

Consider some possible strategies for handling these situations. Remember, you want to respond in ways that are not harmful and

WHAT DO I DO IF ...

Question: I find that it's really hard to change from one activity or class to another, and I feel upset and unable to concentrate and focus when I have to make these types of changes. What do I do?

Answer: Consult your schedule ahead of time so you know exactly what to expect. Most schools run on regular schedules, and they let you know in advance if there are going to be changes. During each class, keep your eyes on the clock so you can remind yourself when the class is going to end. If you can't see the clock, wear a watch that vibrates (avoid buzzers or ring tones, which will disrupt others) and set an alarm for three minutes before each class ends. Ask your teachers for advance warning of any changes, and remind yourself that these changes will occur by writing them down in your planner or calendar. If you are feeling upset during a transition, ask permission to take a short break to get some water or to go to the bathroom. Send yourself reassuring messages that you have handled disruptions and changes before and can do so now.

that can in some cases prevent these triggers from occurring again (although this is not always possible). For each of the three triggers you wrote down, can you think of three strategies for handling the situation? Write them down next to your list of triggers on a separate piece of paper.

IDENTIFYING ALL-OR-NOTHING THINKING

When you read about the common triggers that make many people feel upset, above, you may have recognized that **all-or-nothing thinking** often causes, or contributes to, people feeling overwhelmed. All-or-nothing thinking is an easy pattern to fall into; it means that a person sees a situation in very dire or black-and-white terms without realizing that the situation may not be as drastic or dire as it first seems. Can you identify the all-or-nothing thinking involved in the following examples?

Maria: Maria could not finish her paper because she knew it wasn't as good as the professional writers whose work she read. Even though she spent hours on the paper, she handed it in late and received a poor grade because she had difficulty finishing it.

What is the all-or-nothing thinking?: You may notice that Maria thought a high school paper that wasn't as good as a professional paper wasn't worth handing in to her tenth-grade English teacher. However, papers in high school aren't supposed to be of professional quality. It's all-or-nothing thinking to believe that a high school paper has to either be professional quality or not good enough to submit to a high school English teacher.

Aiden: Aiden decided not to try out for the school band because after listening to his favorite jazz musicians, he knew he wasn't very good.

What is the all-or-nothing thinking?: Like Maria, Aiden believed that if he wasn't a professional-level musician, he could not be part of the school band. However, many—in fact, most—high school musicians are not of professional level, and Aiden can still learn, have fun, and participate in the band even if he is not perfect.

Zoe: When Zoe was new to her high school, she didn't know any other kids. When she tried to get to know kids in her math class, they weren't very friendly. She thought that she would never make friends.

What is the all-or-nothing thinking?: Zoe thought that because she didn't know anyone in her new high school and her first few days were rough, that she would never make friends. She might find that as the days go on, she will find friendly kids, either in class or by joining sports teams or clubs after school. The first few days of school aren't usually representative of what the rest of the school year will be like.

HANDLING CRITICISM

Sometimes, criticism is hard to take, in part because we engage in all-or-nothing thinking. It's easy to think that if someone—whether a parent, teacher, or friend—criticizes you, he or she finds everything wrong with you. However, if you recognize that you may be using all-or-nothing thinking, some forms of criticism that are intended to help you may be easier to accept and to use to make yourself better.

Consider the following example:

Allison kept getting Bs and Cs on her history papers. She didn't really read her teacher's comments, and, instead, she scribbled on the bottom of her paper, "Guess Mr. Watson just hates me!" When her friend received an A, Allison thought it might be because her friend "sucked up to Mr. Watson," in Allison's words. She decided not to read her friend's A paper because, after all, what could Allison do if Mr. Watson liked her friend better? Also, Allison knew she was just "bad at history." She did well on the multiple-choice tests in history, but her essays weren't good. After all, she was good at math, and no one can be good at everything!

What kinds of mistakes has Allison made here? First, she believes that she receives lower grades on her papers just because her teacher doesn't like her, but she hasn't taken the time to read over the comments and figure out if there really is something she could improve to do better. Second, she does not read her friend's A paper to learn how her friend performed better—she just assumes her friend did better because of personal favoritism on the teacher's part. Finally, Allison thinks that even though she does well in some parts of class, that she was just "bad at history" and therefore can't do better. How could Allison handle this type of situation more productively? Here's one scenario:

Allison kept receiving Bs and Cs on her history research papers, even though she generally received As on the multiple-choice tests. She read over her teacher's comments and realized that on each paper, she had not satisfied the teacher's requirement to have a strong thesis statement and at least three outside sources. The next time she wrote a paper, Allison found it hard to approach the teacher, but she did so anyway. She showed the teacher her thesis statement and sources, so the teacher would know how she planned to complete the paper. The teacher made some suggestions, and Allison realized that they weren't intended as criticisms but as ways to improve. As a result, Allison followed the teacher's feedback, and she received an A on her next paper.

In this example, Allison realizes that her teacher's criticism is not intended to be harmful but is instead intended to help her do better. She is able to approach the teacher for help in part because she realizes that she doesn't "suck at history" and that the teacher's criticisms don't mean that she has nothing to offer. As a result, she was able to approach the teacher, hear clearly what the teacher had to say, and respond accordingly, thereby earning a higher grade. Though it was hard to approach the teacher, who seemed scary in class, Allison did so anyway, and she found it wasn't that painful and was definitely helpful!

PERFECTIONISM

Sometimes, all-or-nothing thinking can also lead to **perfectionism,** or thinking that you have to be perfect in order to do something. Perfectionism can affect you in all areas of your life—school, sports, activities, or even making your bed! Your thinking may go something like this: "I'm not doing this right. I'm feeling really frustrated, so I won't do it at all!" The irony about perfectionism—meaning the part of it that turns out the opposite way from what you expect—is that perfectionism can actually prevent you from getting *anything* done. Not only is your work not perfect, but it's actually non-existent. To fight against perfectionism, you can try to realize that you are using all-or-nothing thinking. Just because your work or project isn't perfect, that doesn't mean it's worthless. If you are having trouble finishing projects because of perfectionism, you should speak to a trusted adult.

SENDING YOURSELF HELPFUL MESSAGES

If you are having a hard time handling criticism or just feeling overwhelmed, there are helpful messages, or thoughts, you can send yourself. These messages can remind you that you are using all-or-nothing thinking, that the situation isn't as bad as you thought, and that you have a lot to offer. Try sending yourself one of the following messages:

- Even though my teacher seems to be criticizing me, he is also trying to help me improve my work.
- Even though I didn't do well on this test, I have done better on other tests and can do better on other tests in the future.
- I did poorly on this test, but I am smart. A bad grade on this one test does not mean I'm not smart.
- Even if my work isn't perfect, it's good enough to hand in at this moment.

It may take a while to get the hang of it, but sending messages to yourself can really make a difference in how you feel in difficult or stressful situations.

ASKING FOR HELP WITH EMOTIONS

If you are struggling with feeling sad, negative, depressed, or anxious on a regular basis, you should seek out help from a trusted adult. You may feel that you have to handle everything on your own, but everyone needs to ask others for help sometimes. If you are feeling stuck or very sad, it is particularly important to find a trusted adult who can help you think about how to handle the situation differently.

SETTING GOALS

Now, it's time to set some personal goals about handling emotions, as you might set goals when starting a video game. In order to be attainable, goals have to be SMART in nature; that is, they must be:

Specific,
Measurable,
Attainable,
Realistic, and
Timely.

You might decide on goals such as, "I will bring a sensory tool, such as a squishy ball, that I can fit in my pocket to school this week" or "I will ask my teacher ahead of time if I can get a break if I need one during the school concert," or "I will approach my teacher for feedback on my writing this week and will try to recognize if I am using all-or-nothing thinking if she offers me feedback or what feels like criticism." Your goals are up to you. Try to write down three SMART goals related to handling emotions on a separate sheet of paper.

While you may not always be able to control the situations that arise in high school, some of which can be upsetting, surprising, or overwhelming, you can start to change how you react to—and think about—these types of situations. You can also start to develop new strategies for helping yourself deal with these situations in calm and effective ways.

8

DEVELOPING INDEPENDENCE

High school can be a great time. Your parents and teachers often allow you more independence than you had in middle school, and while this means that you are expected to handle much of your work and responsibilities on your own, it also means you have the ability to do fun things on your own—including choosing who you want to hang out with, where you want to go, and how you get your work and other responsibilities done. Of course, achieving independence does not happen overnight, and your parents may still set limits about where you can go and what you can do. In order to achieve more independence, you may first have to show your parents that you are capable of doing things responsibly on your own.

QUIZ YOURSELF!
HOW WELL DO YOU WORK INDEPENDENTLY?

Here's one last quiz that's all about you. Answer the questions below to assess how well you work independently.

1. When I have to use accommodations in school such as extended time on tests or permission to take breaks, I:
   a. Don't use these types of accommodations, even if I might possibly benefit from them.
   b. Have my parents remind the teacher about these accommodations.
   c. E-mail or speak to my teachers directly to request these types of accommodations.
2. The chores I do at home include:
   a. What chores? That's what parents are for!
   b. Making my bed and setting the table.
   c. Cleaning my own room and doing my own laundry.
3. When I have to go to the doctor, I:
   a. Am reminded of my appointment by my parents, who make it for me.
   b. Remind my parents to make an appointment for me.
   c. Am starting to call to make my own appointments.
4. When it comes to keeping track of my work and appointments, I:
   a. Rely on my parents and my friends.
   b. Use the school website to write down the homework.
   c. Have a planner in which I record schoolwork, appointments, and activities.
5. With regard to my own money, I:
   a. Get an allowance from my parents but don't save most of it.
   b. Get an allowance and try to save some of it to buy things I want.
   c. Am working at a job or trying to get a job to make some extra money, particularly during the summer.

How to score yourself:

If you answered mostly "a": It sounds like you are still relying mostly on your parents to take care of your tasks. As you move towards college or the work world, it's going to be important for you to start taking on some of these responsibilities, as you will soon be on your own. Choose just one or two things you want to start doing independently, such as walking to a nearby friend's house along a route you know, or doing some more chores around the house. Although you may not always enjoy the chores, they will show that you are capable of handling more responsibilities—including fun responsibilities such as going out on your own.

If you answered mostly "b": You are starting to rely on yourself and build practical skills that will help you as you enter college and the work world. It's great that you are beginning to establish your independence in manageable ways, such as going on your own to meet with friends or doing chores. Read on to find some other ways you might continue to develop the skills you are going to need after high school, including making and keeping your own schedule, budgeting your money, and cooking and cleaning for yourself.

If you answered mostly "c": You have many great practical skills and are doing a good job carrying out your work and other responsibilities independently. Read on in this chapter to see if there are other skills you want to develop before heading off to college or the work world.

BECOMING MORE INDEPENDENT

Your job in high school is not only to complete your school work but also to get ready for the next phase in your life—whether it's college or a job. While no one expects you to be fully independent the day you start your freshman year of high school, you want to take some steps each year in high school to move towards being independent and handling the tasks of adulthood on your own. These tasks include the following:

- Handling your own money, whether it's money you've earned from a job or received as part of an allowance.
- Learning how to get from place to place on public transportation and/or how to drive a car.
- Completing tasks on your own, including not only schoolwork but also making doctors' appointments, preparing your own food, doing your own laundry, packing your own bag, and, eventually, even getting your first full-time or part-time job. Being organized also means getting yourself up on your own in the morning.
- Transitioning away from relying on your parents to complete these types of tasks for you.

While it may seem really comfortable to continue to rely on your parents to arrange your appointments, speak with your teachers about what you need, and do your chores, you will one day be responsible for carrying out all these responsibilities on your own. If you don't start practicing some of these skills now, when you are still in high school and can still benefit from the guidance of helpful adults, you may not know what to do when you go out on your own. Learning how to carry out these kinds of tasks on your own is similar to learning how to walk. You may not remember, but when you were a baby or toddler, you started to walk with your parents' help. First, you crawled, and then you held on to nearby objects. Finally, you were ready to walk on your own, but your parents held your hand—tightly at first and then just a little bit as you learned how to balance on your own two feet. If you hadn't taken all these smaller steps, quite literally, you wouldn't have been ready to walk, and later run, on your own. In much the same way, you need to take smaller steps on the way to learning how to live and work on your own after high school—whether you attend college, travel, or work on your own.

WORKING WITH YOUR PARENTS

Your parents can be an important part of helping you develop the skills you need to move towards independence. Like a teacher or sports coach, your parents can be most helpful to you *not* by doing things for you—such as reminding you of the work you have to do or contacting your teachers for you—but by coaching you to do take some of the steps on your own. For example, your parents can show you how to set up a planner system and how to record your work and appointments in the planner. You can even check in with them on a regular basis, whether it is daily or weekly, to put appointments in the planner and make sure you are caught up. However, it is important for you to consult the planner and try to carry out your work and other responsibilities on your own, in addition to these regular check-ups with your parents or other adults.

Similarly, if you work with a tutor, therapist, homework helper, or other kind of support person, this adult can help you develop a planner system or can coach you about how you can complete your work, arrive at appointments on time, and develop other skills. Their job is not to do things for you, as you need practice in working on these skills on your own. Again, the best way to think of supportive adults in your life, whether they are your teachers, parents, or tutors, is that they are coaches. They will show you ways to accomplish work on your own, and you can change around what they show you if you would like. Just as athletes have to play in the game themselves while coaches watch, support, and advise them on the sidelines, you have to complete your own work with adults' support and advice.

GETTING ORGANIZED

The most critical step you can take in moving towards independence and arranging your life with only minimal support from your parents is working out some kind of organizational system. In the chapter entitled "Working with Teachers and Completing Work," you can find more information about how to set up and use a planner or organizational system in which you record your assignments. You also can use this system to record other types of appointments you have, such as sports games, after-school activities, doctors' appointments, etc. Using this system will help you become more independent from your parents.

Again, you can check in with your parents, teachers, or other adults to make sure you have recorded everything you need to in your planner, but it will become up to you to use the planner and look at it daily to remind yourself on what you need to do. One idea is for you to look at your planner each night, before you get ready for bed. That way, you will know what to expect each day, and you can pack your own bag with the right things. For example, if you have a sports game the next day, you will need your uniform and sneakers. If you have an arts class, you will need to pack your materials, and your parents won't need to remind you. To prepare for life after high school, you should eventually also learn how to get up on your own in the morning—without having to rely on your parents to get you out of bed.

One way to get more organized is to look at your planner each night, before you go to bed.

If you find that you are constantly forgetting what you need to bring to school, try taping a checklist on your mirror or some other place you are sure to look in the morning. For example, the checklist could read:

CHECKLIST FOR THE MORNING:
-bring lunch from fridge
-bring planner
-bring uniform for sports
-pack calculator

WHAT DO I DO IF ...

Question: I know I can do better at school, but I can't keep track of my homework. What do I do?

Answer: Even though you may have a great deal to contribute to class and to your assignments, handing your work in on time is part of your grade in high school. In order to receive full credit, you are going to have to come up with a system to write down each assignment and its due date. (For more information, see Chapter 2, "Working with Teachers and Completing Work.") You have to get used to looking at your assignment book and breaking your longer-term assignments down into smaller tasks so that you can finish your larger assignments on time. If you have trouble, ask a teacher or parent to help you plan your work. If you find you don't use or remember to use a paper planner, you can write your assignments on a large wall calendar or dry-erase board on your wall. Post the calendar where you are likely to look at it, and use different colors for different tasks or subjects so that you remember them more clearly. Try to keep your papers in one large binder or accordion folder with different compartments for different subjects so you won't have to keep track of multiple folders.

That way, you are sure to remind yourself of what to bring, and you don't need to rely on your parents. While it may seem easier to have your parents remind you, remember that with their reminders, they may also nag you. It may, in fact, be easier and more comfortable for you to carry out these tasks than to have your parents constantly nag you to do so. If you develop your ability to do things on your own, your parents may be more likely to allow you to do fun things on your own, too, such as go out with friends.

ASSESSING YOUR PRACTICAL SKILLS

These are the types of skills you should have by the time you graduate from high school. For each skill, note if you can carry it out on your own, carry it out with some help from adults, or if you can't carry it out yet.

Money Skills

I can earn money by babysitting, mowing lawns, or working at another job:
 a. I can do this.
 b. I can carry this out with some support, such as my parents helping me to find babysitting or yard work.
 c. I cannot do this yet.

I can make up and carry out a plan to save money to buy something I want.
 a. I can do this.
 b. I can do this with some support.
 c. I cannot do this yet.

I have my own bank account and know how to make deposits, take out money from an ATM, and keep a minimum balance.

    a. I can do this.

    b. I can do this with some support.

    c. I cannot do this yet.

I know how to keep my money safe by keeping my bank card and cash in a safe place and shopping at secure websites:

    a. I can do this.

    b. I can do this with some support.

    c. I cannot do this yet.

Transportation Skills

I can get to my friends' houses by walking, driving, or using a bus or other means of public transportation:

    a. I can do this.

    b. I can do this with some support.

    c. I cannot do this yet.

If I stay after school, I can get home on my own.

    a. I can do this.

    b. I can do this with some support.

    c. I cannot do this yet.

If I want to go shopping, I can find the store and go on my own or with friends:

    a. I can do this.

    b. I can do this with some support, such as my parents directing me to the store.

    c. I cannot do this yet.

Working With Adults

If I have a problem with an assignment or task such as following directions in gym class, I can speak to the teacher directly:
    a. I can do this.
    b. I can do this with some support, such as my parents helping me write the teacher an e-mail that I send and follow up on my own.
    c. I cannot do this yet.

If I need an accommodation such as extra time on a test or permission to take a break, I can ask my teacher directly for this accommodation:
    a. I can do this.
    b. I can do this with some support, such as my parents helping me write an e-mail or coaching me about how to speak with my teacher.
    c. I cannot do this yet.

I can be responsible for checking my e-mail each day at school or at home to be sure to respond to e-mails from teachers or other adults at school.
    a. I can do this.
    b. I can do this with some support, such as my parents reminding me to check my e-mail.
    c. I cannot do this yet.

Household Skills

I can cook a few meals on my own:
    a. I can do this.
    b. I can do this with some support, such as my parents helping me with some of the steps involved in making a recipe.
    c. I cannot do this yet.

I can do my own laundry:
- a. I can do this.
- b. I can do this with some support, such as my parents giving me a list of the directions I can follow.
- c. I cannot do this yet.

I can carry out household cleaning chores, such as vacuuming, clearing off the table, and washing dishes or loading the dishwasher:
- a. I can do this.
- b. I can do this with some support, such as my parents reminding me how to vacuum or load the dishwasher.
- c. I cannot do this yet.

Organizational Skills

I can organize my own planner and appointments.
- a. I can do this.
- b. I can do this with some support, such as checking in with teachers or parents to see if I have everything in my planner.
- c. I cannot do this yet.

I can get myself up in the morning on my own.
- a. I can do this.
- b. I can do this with some support; for example, I set my own alarm, but my parents make sure I am up.
- c. I cannot do this yet.

I can pack my own school bag with what I need for the day:
- a. I can do this.
- b. I can do this with some support, such as checking in with my parents to make sure I have everything.
- c. I cannot do this yet.

From the list above, choose 2–3 skills you would like to develop, either from among the skills you cannot do yet or from among the skills you can do with some help. Below are some ways you can improve these skills.

DEVELOPING PRACTICAL SKILLS

Here are some ideas about how to develop these skills:

Money Skills

- Ask your parents to help you set up a budget. For example, they might start you off with $25 in cash or on a pre-paid debit card, and you can be responsible for planning out your expenses for the next week or so and paying for your expenses.
- Learn how to use your bank's services, including checking your account balance (the amount left in your account) online with a secure password that you set up, withdrawing money from an ATM, depositing money or checks in an ATM, and understanding the interest that accrues on your money. Store your banking card in a safe place, and be sure to return it to your wallet or pocket after you use it. Make sure you know how to cancel your card if you lose it.
- If you are saving for an expensive item, work with your parents to set up a savings account at your bank. Make regular deposits, and ask your parents to explain how your account will earn interest, or money that accrues on savings.
- If you have time during the school year or summer, you can look for a part-time job, such as babysitting, mowing lawns, or doing odd jobs. Start by asking neighbors or family friends if they need help. If you are interested in babysitting, consider enrolling in a course given in your community by Safe Sitter at http://www.safesitter.org to learn how to watch children safely.

Transportation Skills

- Start by choosing a new destination near your house, such as a store or friend's house. Plan out your route ahead of time, either by foot or by public transportation. Ask your parents how to get the right kind of card or change to use on the bus and which stop to get off at, and let your parents know you arrived safely by calling or texting them. Agree in advance when you will come home.

- If possible, work on getting home from school on your own if you cannot take the school bus or miss the bus. That means you should figure out the route ahead of time using public transportation.

- When taking public transportation, know where to get off in advance, and do not speak to strangers. Once you board a bus or train, store your money and cards in a safe place. Listen carefully to announcements, and ask the driver or conductor if you have any questions or problems.

Working With Adults

- Please see Chapter 2, "Working with Teachers and Completing Work." You should be able to ask your teachers for help if you are confused about how to write a paper, study for test, or follow directions or steps in a task. You should be able to do this without asking your parents to do it for you. However, a parent or trusted adult can coach you about how to approach the teacher *yourself* to ask for help.

- You should also be responsible for checking your school e-mail regularly and for responding to e-mails from teachers and other adults in a timely way, meaning in the time they expect you to respond.

Household Skills

- Have your parents show you how to do a load of laundry, and then offer to do the family laundry—or at least your own. It's relatively easy, and you will endear yourself to your parents and learn a helpful skill in the process.
- Make sure you know how to pick out an appropriate outfit for school and for events such as parties, interviews, or formal events. Ask your parents if you need help, but get your clothes and shoes together yourself.
- Learn a few easy dishes that you can make, such as pasta, baked chicken, pancakes, eggs, etc. Ask your parents to teach you rules for cooking safely, including turning off the stove and microwave when you are finished, using pot holders to remove hot dishes from the oven, and rules for using a microwave.
- Learn how to shop for groceries and how to compare prices and plan a weekly menu on a budget. You can plan a menu in advance and go to a local grocery store and choose items with a parent. Then, check if your items are under or over your allotted budget. If they are over budget, ask your parent for help in staying within your limit.
- Try Cooking with Autism at http://www.cookingwithautism.com. This helpful website explains how to follow recipes. These recipes have been tested by teens with Asperger's and autism, who have determined that they are easy to follow. They also publish a cookbook with their recipes.

Organizational Skills

- For more information on setting up an organizational system to keep track of your schoolwork, please see Chapter 2, "Working with Teachers and Completing Work."

- Work with your parents or teachers to set up an organizational system or planner that you fill out, not just for your schoolwork, but also to keep track of after-school activities, social events, and other appointments. You can check in with teachers or parents to see that you have entered all the information, but it's your responsibility to consult your schedule and fill in the necessary information.
- Learn how to set up your own alarm in the morning in a way that makes you get out of bed without your parents needing to step in. Getting up and out on your own is a vital skill for life after high school, when you are in college or getting to a job each day.
- Start packing your own bag each day before you go to school. Use a checklist posted on your wall or mirror if you tend to forget items.

Even though your parents may help you out with these tasks now, developing some practical skills in each of these categories will prepare you to live independently and make your transition to college or work life easier.

MARK'S STORY

Mark thought his parents were great because they did everything for him, so he could just concentrate on getting his schoolwork done. When he had to go to the doctor, they made an appointment for him, and if he had a teacher he didn't get along with, they e-mailed the teacher to see what the teacher, not Mark, could do differently. When he had to study for a test, his mother sat with him and helped him review, and she also reminded him to hand in assignments and even helped him get out of bed in the morning. As a result, Mark did well enough in high school to get into a good college. When Mark went to college, he brought his laptop, video games, mini-fridge, spending money from his parents, and clothes. There were two critical things he left at home—his mom and dad! When he had trouble with his professor during his first semester, his parents weren't there to e-mail the professor and figure out the problem. In addition, the professor didn't respond to e-mails from parents! Mark regularly forgot to check his school e-mail, so he did not respond to his professors or deans, and he missed the deadlines for signing up for several classes. It was Mark's responsibility to keep track of his assignments, but he had trouble organizing himself to hand in long papers and study for tests on his own. He also had a hard time getting up in the morning and slept through many classes. In addition, he ran out of money after two weeks, even though the money was supposed to last him all semester! Finally, he went around in dirty clothes because he had never learned how to do laundry and was too embarrassed to ask.

Wow. Maybe you are asking yourself how Mark could've let the situation get so bad. Who wants to be smelly during a time when they are meeting new people at college? Well, Mark was because there was no one to do his laundry for him. How could Mark have prevented this situation? He might have taken the following steps in high school:

- He needed to learn how to keep track of his own assignments and prepare for tests on his own, without relying on his mom and dad.
- He needed to learn to get up on his own, without his parents' help.
- When he had a problem with a teacher or assignment, he needed to learn how to approach the teacher politely and how to accept what the teacher said.

- Mark needed to learn how to be responsible for checking his school e-mail and responding to e-mails from teachers in a timely way.
- Mark needed to learn how to budget his money and come up with a list of expenses so he wouldn't run out of money.
- Mark definitely needed to learn how to do his laundry before heading to college.

Mark's story might be a drastic one, but it shows how much easier it is to start developing practical skills *before* you leave home, rather than when you are already at college or living on your own while working. If you feel that you have not reached a level of independence by college, you and your parents may need to research colleges that provide more support in these areas, such as colleges that have counselors who will work with you to choose your classes, structure your time, and even help you connect with other students. If you are interested in finding out more about these programs, you can consult the college guidance counselor at your school.

SETTING GOALS

Now, it's time to set some personal goals about developing independence, as you might set goals when starting a video game. In order to be attainable, goals have to be SMART in nature; that is, they must be:

Specific,
Measurable,
Attainable,
Realistic, and
Timely.

You might set goals such as, "In the next week, I will go to the mall on my own using the bus," or "I will try putting all my after-school activities in my planner, so I don't have to ask my parents about them," or "I will ask my parents to help me set up a savings account this week so I can begin to save towards something I want to buy."

Your goals are up to you. Try to write down three SMART goals on a separate sheet of paper.

High school students do not become independent overnight, and you are not expected to do everything on your own right now, but by starting to develop and carry out your chosen goals, you are now on your way to developing more independence for high school—and for life afterward.

GLOSSARY

Accommodations: Changes in the school day that can help you function better, such as receiving additional time on tests or the use of a computer for writing.

All-or-nothing thinking: Also known as **black-and-white thinking,** this type of mental process involves thinking about a situation in extreme terms without considering other possible solutions or alternatives. For example, if you receive a poor grade on one test, all-or-nothing thinking might result in your thinking you will fail the course rather than that you might improve on the next test. In other words, there are always many alternative outcomes or solutions to a situation or problem, and you should not consider only the worst one.

Bibliography: The list of sources a student uses in writing a paper or completing a project. It is important to know how to format a bibliography and cite the sources you use in a paper correctly.

Body language: The way in which people hold their bodies, which sends messages to the people they are speaking to.

Bullying: Making someone else feel uncomfortable or unwanted in school or attacking them physically, verbally, or through e-mail (or other forms of communication such as texts or posts on social networking sites). It can also include spreading rumors about another person. Bullying is illegal in most U.S. states.

Cliques: Social groups that may include or exclude other people.

Comfort zone: A place or range of places in which you feel at ease, both physically and emotionally.

Cyberbullying: Harassing others through e-mail, social networking sites, text messages, and other forms of electronic technology. Like other forms of bullying, it is illegal in most U.S. states.

Etiquette: Rules about how to behave in social situations.

Fine motor skills: Using small muscles in activities such as writing, handling smaller objects, or buttoning clothing. These types of activities may be difficult for some people with Asperger's.

Gross motor skills: Using larger muscles to carry out activities such as kicking, sitting, running, or walking. These types of activities may be difficult for some people with Asperger's, though certainly not all.

Perfectionism: Telling yourself that you can't do or finish something unless it is perfect. This type of thinking often prevents you or slows you down from finishing what you start.

Plagiarism: The act of using other people's ideas as one's own either by copying their ideas or by writing them down directly without crediting them. This practice is not allowed, so you should be sure to ask your teachers how to cite other works when writing papers or doing other assignments.

Profile: A list of a person's skills, strengths, and weaknesses.

Sensory input: Information that comes through your five senses (hearing, sight, touch, taste, and smell). Some people with Asperger's react strongly to sensory input such as loud noises, bright lights, or strong smells.

Sensory tool: A squishy or soft toy that you can use to calm your senses and feel more relaxed.

Sexual identity: Whether a person likes people of the same or opposite sex (or both) and how they think of themselves.

Stim behaviors: Short for "stimulation behaviors." Repetitive motions such as clapping, waving, jumping, or other actions that some people with Asperger's use to calm themselves.

Syllabus: The list of assignments and course expectations that teachers sometimes hand out, usually at the beginning of the school year or of the course. Teachers may also distribute a list of assignments and due dates throughout the year or course.

Trigger: An event or person that sets off an emotion in another person. Some triggers can be positive, while others result in negative emotions.

Tone: The way your writing or speaking sounds to other people. To use a polite tone, address a person correctly and say thank you. Consider whether you are speaking clearly and calmly. Your tone is conveyed by the way in which you speak—not just your words.

Visualizing: Using a method of relaxation in which you imagine a peaceful scene in your mind.

RESOURCES

On Asperger's

OASIS: http://www.aspergersyndrome.org
OASIS provides a teacher's guide to help you explain Asperger's. They also provide information and resources to help people with Asperger's Syndrome.

Wrong Planet: http://www.wrongplanet.net
An online community for people with Asperger's. Ask your parents' permission before joining.

Your Little Professor: http://www.yourlittleprofessor.com
On this site, you can find resources and articles to help kids and teens with Asperger's.

Other Helpful Websites

Cooking With Autism: http://www.cookingwithautism.com
This helpful website explains how to follow recipes that have been tested by teens with Asperger's and autism, who have determined that they are easy to follow. They also publish a cookbook with their recipes.

Fact Sheets—Underage Drinking: http://www.cdc.gov/alcohol/fact-sheets/underage-drinking.htm
This site gives you the facts about underage drinking.

On-line Gamers Anonymous: http://www.olganon.org
This is the site of a self-help organization to help people whose lives have been taken over by gaming.

Quizlet: http://www.quizlet.com
This free site allows you to create index cards to quiz yourself and includes other online study tools.

Safe Sitter: http://www.safesitter.org
This organization provides classes in many local communities for teenagers so they can watch younger kids safely.

Stopbullying.gov: http://www.stopbullying.gov/
This site provides information about how to stop bullying in school, your community, and online.

BOOKS

About Asperger's

Attwood, T. (2008). *The complete guide to Asperger's syndrome.* London, UK: Jessica Kingsley.
> This encyclopedic guide to Asperger's is intended for people with Asperger's, as well as their families and people, such as therapists, who work with them.

Grandin, T. (2010). *Thinking in pictures: My life with autism.* New York, NY: Vintage.
> The author is a famous animal scientist and autism activist who talks about the way some people with autism see the world.

Grossberg, B. (2012). *Asperger's rules!: How to make sense of school and friends.* Washington, DC: Magination Press.
> This is a book to help middle school students with Asperger's understand how to navigate the challenges of school.

Robison, J. E. (2008). *Look me in the eye: My life with Asperger's.* New York, NY: Three Rivers Press.

>The author, who has a great sense of humor and an entertaining writing style, discusses his childhood with undiagnosed Asperger's and his adulthood, which he has spent designing customized guitars and cars.

Welton, J. (2002). *Can I tell you about Asperger syndrome?: A guide for friends and family.* London, UK: Jessica Kingsley.

>This book is intended to help younger kids understand and explain Asperger's to friends, teachers, and family members.

On Dating

Fox, A. (2005). *The teen survival guide to dating & relating: Real-world advice for teens on guys, girls, growing up, and getting along.* Minneapolis, MN: Free Spirit.

>The book is out of print but is available as a free download on the author's website, http://www.anniefox.com. The author of this book helps you think about what you want in your relationships with other people and the importance of respecting yourself. The book also helps people who are thinking about their sexual identity, meaning whether they like people of the same or opposite sex (or both) and how they think about themselves.

Huegel, K. (2011). *GLBTQ: The survival guide for gay, lesbian, bisexual, transgender, and questioning teens.* (2nd ed.). Minneapolis, MN: Free Spirit.

>Also available as a Kindle edition. This book addresses questions of sexual identity.

INDEX